JOHN McCAIN

Recent Titles in Greenwood Biographies

JOHN McCAIN

A Biography

Elaine S. Povich

GREENWOOD BIOGRAPHIES

GREENWOOD PRESS
WESTPORT, CONNECTICUT • LONDON

Library of Congress Cataloging-in-Publication Data

Povich, Elaine S.
  John McCain : a biography / Elaine S. Povich.
    p. cm. — (Greenwood biographies, ISSN 1540–4900)
  Includes bibliographical references and index.
  ISBN 978–0–313–36252–1 (alk. paper)
  1. McCain, John, 1936–   2. Legislators—United States—Biography.
3. United States. Congress. Senate—Biography.   4. Presidential
candidates—United States—Biography.   I. Title.
  E840.8.M26P68   2009
  973.931092—dc22
  [B]   2008045044

British Library Cataloguing in Publication Data is available.

Library of Congress Catalog Card Number: 2008045044
ISBN: 978–0–313–36252–1
ISBN: 978–1–4408–3598–8 (pbk.)
ISSN: 1540–4900

First published in 2009

Greenwood Press, 88 Post Road West, Westport, CT 06881
An imprint of Greenwood Publishing Group, Inc.
www.greenwood.com

Printed in the United States of America

The paper used in this book complies with the
Permanent Paper Standard issued by the National
Information Standards Organization (Z39.48–1984).

10 9 8 7 6 5 4 3 2 1

For Mom and the memory of Dad, who disagreed with John McCain on many issues but liked him anyway.
For Mark and Kenny, who are on their way to achieving something greater than their self-interest. And with loving admiration for Ron, who achieved it long ago and continues to do so every day.

CONTENTS

CONTENTS

Photo essay follows page 84

SERIES FOREWORD

In response to high school and public library needs, Greenwood developed this distinguished series of full-length biographies specifically for student use. Prepared by field experts and professionals, these engaging biographies are tailored for high school students who need challenging yet accessible biographies. Ideal for secondary school assignments, the length, format and subject areas are designed to meet educators' requirements and students' interests.

Greenwood offers an extensive selection of biographies spanning all curriculum-related subject areas including social studies, the sciences, literature and the arts, history and politics, as well as popular culture, covering public figures and famous personalities from all time periods and backgrounds, both historic and contemporary, who have made an impact on American and/or world culture. Greenwood biographies were chosen based on comprehensive feedback from librarians and educators. Consideration was given to both curriculum relevance and inherent interest. The result is an intriguing mix of the well known and the unexpected, the saints and sinners from long-ago history and contemporary pop culture. Readers will find a wide array of subject choices from fascinating crime figures like Al Capone to inspiring pioneers like Margaret Mead, from the greatest minds of our time like Stephen Hawking to the most amazing success stories of our day like J. K. Rowling.

While the emphasis is on fact, not glorification, the books are meant to be fun to read. Each volume provides in-depth information about the subject's life from birth through childhood, the teen years, and adulthood.

A thorough account relates family background and education, traces personal and professional influences, and explores struggles, accomplishments, and contributions. A timeline highlights the most significant life events against a historical perspective. Bibliographies supplement the reference value of each volume.

ACKNOWLEDGMENTS

Every author is indebted to those who came before. This book benefited from the work of several writers, not the least of whom are John McCain himself and his talented co-author, Mark Salter. Together, McCain and Salter have written five books, including two that chronicle much of McCain's life, *Faith of My Fathers* and *Worth the Fighting For*. I am grateful for the vivid detail contained in these books and to the man who remembered them in "Technicolor" and "surround sound."

Writer Bob Timberg's *The Nightingale's Song* and *John McCain: An American Odyssey* provided in-depth information on McCain gleaned from years of hard work and a special affinity that is the product of their both being graduates of the U.S. Navy Academy. Paul Alexander's *Man of the People: The Life of John McCain* is a finely detailed portrait.

The *Arizona Republic's* 14-part series on McCain by Dan Nowicki and Bill Muller was the most detailed chronology of any I consulted.

I am also grateful for the support and counsel of many friends, sources, and associates who provided insight and sounding boards during the writing of this book. I would like to thank Jim Toedtman, who first assigned me to the McCain 2000 campaign when we both were working for *Newsday* and who provided unstinting encouragement.

Roberta McCain and Joe McCain provided reminiscences of their nomadic Navy family life and stories about their son and brother, respectively, that could have come from no other sources. They were generous with their time, pictures, and memories.

Frank Gamboa shared tales of the Naval Academy and provided insights into the character and temperament of his roommate. Naomi Belisle and

Morele Rosenfeld recalled the days of John McCain as a young, dashing naval aviator. Former Vietnam POW Orson Swindle regaled late-night McCain bus riders with stories of imprisonment and valor that made better telling than they could ever have made living. The horrors were pushed into the background; the heroism and camaraderie remained.

I am indebted to former colleagues Monica Norton and Angela Johnson, to David Cassidy at the Newsday Library, and to the staff of the U.S. Senate Library for quick and precise research.

It is a great compliment to John McCain that those who have worked most closely with him are eager to talk about the experience. I am grateful to Mark Salter, John Weaver, Todd Harris, Lanny Wiles, Howard Opinsky, Jay Smith, Torie Clark, and others for sharing insights into the man for whom they worked. Brittany Bramell, logistical genius, helped coordinate my contacts with McCain 2008. Former senators William Cohen and Warren Rudman shared unrivaled personal insights and professional acumen.

Thanks to my editors at National Journal's *CongressDaily*, especially Kathy Gambrell, Keith White, and Lou Peck, for supporting me and this project.

I am greatly indebted to friends in and out of journalism who provided guidance and perspective. Marie Cocco, good friend, great reporter and ace columnist, was there to talk through the tough times. Steve Daley shared contacts, gave writing style pointers, and provided inspiration. I am grateful for the journalistic suggestions of Jack Torry, accomplished author and storyteller. A very personal thanks to Sharon Kaufman, still the best best friend ever, for cheering me on.

Thanks are due to Sandy Towers of Greenwood Publishing Group for persuading me to take on this project when I had barely caught my breath from the last one and for giving me guidance and encouragement throughout.

And, above all, I am grateful for and awed by the ability of my extraordinary husband, Ron Dziengiel, and my very special sons, Mark and Kenny Dziengiel, to accommodate me and to carry on seamlessly (beach trip, family movie nights, and countless restaurant meals) while I was consumed by the writing of this book.

Finally, my thanks to the singular John McCain, whose one-of-a-kind, still-unfinished life story, were it written as fiction, might be dismissed as implausible. But it has the extra added advantage of being true.

INTRODUCTION

October 26, 1967—The missile looked like a flying telephone pole. And John McCain knew it was coming for him. A shrill tone, warning that a missile was about to hit his A-4 Skyhawk aircraft, was urgently sounding. But his mission was to bomb a North Vietnamese power plant, and he figured he had just enough time to drop the bombs and get away. He figured wrong. Just as he pulled back on the stick to release the bombs, the surface-to-air missile slammed into his airplane—BAM!—blowing off the right wing.

Instantly, he reached for the ejection lever. There wasn't time to think.

"My training said, if you are hit this badly, eject," McCain remembered. "It was a good thing I did when I did, because my plane was spiraling straight down."[1]

He broke both his arms and his right leg at the knee from the force of the ejection and parachuted into a lake in downtown Hanoi, the North Vietnamese capital. He was dragged out by Vietnamese citizens. For the next five and a half years, he would be a prisoner of war. His injuries were never properly treated. He was tortured and kept in squalid conditions and spent two years of that time in solitary.

His life would be forever changed by the experience. The independent, devil-may-care pilot would come to depend on others for his food, health—and his very life.

But his core of independence, rebelliousness, and stubbornness would keep him alive and save him for another purpose, a purpose, as he so often put it, "greater than self-interest." His terrible circumstances might have killed a lesser spirit. But not McCain.

John Sidney McCain III was born to a life in the Navy. Both his father and grandfather were Navy admirals, and it was predetermined that he would go to the Naval Academy and become a naval officer. He might have continued on that path to become part of the first three-generation admiral family, but fate intervened.

He survived the Vietnam War and went on to a different career, still in public service but now in the civilian world. He served in the U.S. House and the U.S. Senate. Then the highest civilian calling of all—president of the United States—called to him.

It was almost as if surviving his precarious life was a message that he had been saved for a reason. There were so many times he survived.

He survived not only the Vietnam shoot-down and the horrible POW experience but also a devastating fire on the USS *Forrestal,* an aircraft carrier, which killed 134 of his comrades. He survived two other airplane crashes in which he had to eject. He survived lesser accidents in cars and planes. He survived one failed marriage but found love in another. Along the way, he managed to keep the love of seven children.

He survived a lapse of judgment and a minor rebuke from the Senate in the Keating Five scandal, which took down other senators. He survived scurrilous attacks on his character, his temperament, his valor, and his family in his first race for president.

Every time he was left for dead—physically or politically—he managed to come back. A cat's "nine lives" are nothing compared to the lives of John McCain.

He says he learned perseverance from his parents, John "Jack" McCain Jr. and Roberta Wright McCain. Perhaps he got more of it from his mother, who, forced to move around the country and the world following a Navy officer, always made the best of things. McCain was self-indulgent for much of his early life but always persevered. He developed a tough skin, a ready fist, and a hot temper when necessary.

Age tempered those streaks but did not extinguish them. While more measured in his conduct as a politician and officeholder, he still could lash out at what he felt was unfairness or simply wrong.

His path to power was not an easy one. Sometimes his own failings got in the way. Sometimes it was fate. He never envisioned himself as a political leader early in his life. But he became an effective one.

The man who was born in the Panama Canal Zone (U.S. territory) and who had gone to 20 different schools during the course of his childhood found a home in Arizona, the home state of his second wife, Cindy. He grew to love it—he called it "my beautiful Arizona" with the red hills and canyons—and became emotional at times about finally having roots.

When McCain began to see that he might become president of the United States, there must have been something in him that bordered on disbelief. He pointed to his failings often, noting that he finished near the bottom of his class at the Naval Academy and dismissing descriptions of "heroism" with the line that it didn't take much talent or heroism to "intercept a Soviet-made surface-to-air missile with my own airplane."

He called people "jerks," or worse, but always with affection. A wicked sense of humor kept him real about himself. His response to questions about his age and numerous physical impairments was another often-used line: "I'm older than dirt and have more scars than Frankenstein." But he also had an iron constitution and an ability to be completely refreshed after a catnap on an airplane.

When he lost his first run for the presidency, McCain pronounced himself satisfied with his life and career. But he had tasted a bit of the top prize, and when he embarked on another run for the highest civilian office in the land, he did so with ambition, as well as humility.

When he ran a second time, again he faltered, at first. He tried to run a campaign like a front-runner, which he was for a time. But that campaign soon ran out of money and lost its way. So, with a shoestring budget and a shrunken staff, he righted himself and persevered. And he became the nominee of his party by adhering to the principles that had been with him for the better part of his life—serving something greater than himself, in his case, his country.

"I learned long ago that serving only oneself is a petty and unsatisfying ambition. But serve a cause greater than self-interest and you will know a happiness far more sublime than the fleeting pleasure of fame and fortune. For me that greater cause has always been my country, which I have served imperfectly for many years, but have loved without any reservation every day of my life."[2]

NOTES

1. John McCain, interview with author, July 25, 2008, Washington, DC.

2. John McCain, remarks on winning the New Hampshire primary, January 8, 2008, Nashua, NH, John McCain for President Web site.

TIMELINE OF EVENTS IN THE LIFE OF JOHN McCAIN

November 2, 1982	Elected as Republican to House of Representatives.
October 23, 1984	Daughter Meghan born.
November 6, 1984	Re-elected to House.
May 2, 1986	Son John Sidney "Jack" McCain IV born.
November 4	Elected to Senate, replacing retiring Senator Barry Goldwater.
April 2, 1987	Meets with federal regulators on behalf of developer Charles Keating, who is being investigated by the Federal Home Loan Bank Board.
May 21, 1988	Son James "Jimmy" McCain born.
August 1991	Cited for "poor judgment" by Senate Ethics Committee in Keating affair.
November 3, 1992	Re-elected to Senate with 58 percent of vote despite Keating scandal.
1993	Daughter Bridget, then age 2 (born July 21, 1991), adopted from Bangladesh.
1997	Becomes chairman of powerful Senate Commerce Committee.
November 3, 1998	Re-elected to third term in Senate.
December 30	Establishes exploratory committee to seek GOP presidential nomination in 2000.
April 14, 1999	Declares himself a candidate for the White House.
September 27	Formally announces campaign; tours New Hampshire aboard "Straight Talk Express" bus.
February 1, 2000	Wins New Hampshire primary by 19 points in stunning upset.
February 19	Loses South Carolina primary after weeks of negative ads aired.
March 9	Suspends campaign after losing most of "Super Tuesday" primaries to George Bush.
August	Treated for melanoma, a serious form of skin cancer.
March 27, 2002	President Bush signs Bipartisan Campaign Finance Reform act, known as "McCain-Feingold" law.
November 4, 2004	Elected to fourth term in Senate.
November 15, 2006	Forms exploratory committee for 2008 White House campaign.
February 28, 2007	Announces on CBS's *Late Night with David Letterman* that he will seek 2008 GOP nomination for president.

April 24	Formally announces 2008 White House run.
January 8, 2008	Wins New Hampshire primary.
January 19	Wins South Carolina primary
March 4	Clinches Republican nomination for president.
November 2	Loses presidency to Barack Obama.

Sources: John McCain for President Web site, http://www.johnmccain.com/McCainTimeline/, *Des Moines Register, New York Times, Democracy in Action.*

Chapter 1

SON AND GRANDSON
OF ADMIRALS

The first memory John Sidney McCain III had of his father was of him leaving to fight a war.

It was December 7, 1941, a date, said President Franklin Delano Roosevelt, "that will live in infamy."[1] John McCain was five years old.

He recalled that Sunday morning, playing in the front yard of his family's home in New London, Connecticut, where his father, John Sidney McCain Jr., nicknamed "Jack," was a submarine commander. Suddenly, a black car passing the home slowed down, and the driver, a Navy officer, shouted out of the window, "Jack, the Japs have bombed Pearl Harbor!" using the word for Japanese that was common at the time. The United States was now in World War II.

"My father left for the base immediately," McCain wrote in his book *Faith of My Fathers*. "I saw very little of him for the next four years."[2]

That was the life of the Navy family into which John McCain was born. Not only was his father a Navy admiral, but so too was his grandfather, John Sidney "Slew" McCain. If there was a family business for the McCains, the Navy was it.

It wasn't always that way. Before the first John Sidney McCain went to the Naval Academy, the McCains and their ancestors were Army men. But, no matter what branch of the service, the military seemed to be in their blood, and war was its defining characteristic. War would play a pivotal role in McCain's life and that of his father and grandfather, as it had for generations before them in the McCain family.

McCains served in every American war, beginning with the American Revolution, in 1776. They served on the side of the Confederacy in the Civil War, as several McCain relatives were from Mississippi, and the family had a presence there into the twenty-first century. Camp McCain, in Grenada, Mississippi, was named for Major General Henry Pinckney McCain, a relative and another West Pointer, known as the father of the military draft because he organized it in World War I.

The McCains married into the Young family, McCain wrote in his book, and the Youngs had an even more distinguished military history, if that's possible. The Youngs arrived in America before the McCains, coming from Scotland in 1646 when Mary Young Lamont crossed the Irish Sea after her husband, Sir James Lamont, and his clansmen were defeated in battle by Archibald Campbell, the eighth Duke of Argyle. After that war, Sir James's wife fled into Ireland and took the name Young.

By 1764, Hugh Young, a descendant, had immigrated to Augusta County, Virginia. Hugh's son, John, came to the attention of George Washington and joined Washington's staff.

John's son, David Young, was a captain in the army and fought in the War of 1812. David's son, John William Young, fought for the Confederacy.

The fifth of David Young's eight children, Elizabeth Ann, married McCain's great-grandfather, yet another John Sidney McCain. Elizabeth Ann and John had a plantation and probably owned slaves. John Sidney "Slew" McCain was born to Elizabeth Ann and John on August 9, 1884, and attended high school in Carrollton, Mississippi, then attended the University of Mississippi. But, after one year, it was off to the Naval Academy in Annapolis.

Meanwhile, "Slew" McCain's brother, William Alexander McCain, was a West Point cavalry officer who had chased the Mexican revolutionary General Pancho Villa in 1916 with Pershing and served as an artillery officer in World War I, rising to brigadier general in the Quartermaster Corps.[3]

"It is a formidable history, not easily escaped even today by descendants who might wish to pursue some interest outside the family business," McCain wrote in his autobiography.[4]

If there was any kind of ancestral home for the McCains in America, it was Carroll County, Mississippi, which was the family seat since 1848. The last McCain to live on the plantation property, called Teoc, after a Choctaw Indian name that means "Tall Pines," was McCain's grandfather's brother, Joe McCain.

McCain spent several summers with his Uncle Joe and "enjoyed it immensely. I had never had a permanent address because my father's naval career required us to move frequently. But here, in the care of my very likeable Uncle Joe, I could imagine, with a little envy, what it must have been like for the McCains who came before me to be so connected to one place; to be part of a community and a landscape as well as a family."[5]

But his path was to travel around the country and the world as the grandson and son of a Navy admiral.

"SLEW"

"Slew" McCain fought his war, won his war, came home, and died. He lived long enough to witness the surrender of the Japanese on the deck of the battleship USS *Missouri*. He had risen through the Navy to command the Carrier Task Force of the Third Fleet in World War II, started out as a less than average seaman at the Naval Academy, a performance that belied his innate ability to command men. He graduated in the bottom quarter of his class, ranking 79 out of 116,[6] (a "feat" that would be topped—or bottomed—by both his son and his grandson) but was described as popular and fun-loving in his 1906 yearbook.[7]

In World War I, McCain served on the armored cruiser San Diego, escorting wartime convoys across the Atlantic, through lines of German U-boats (submarines)—harrowing duty that steeled him for his future warfare commands.[8]

He recognized early that flying was becoming essential to the Navy and to warfare at sea. He complied with the Navy's directives that all commanders learn how to fly, but, as his grandson tells the story, he never got very good at it. What he was good at, however, was taking whatever the pilots dished out. When riding in the back seat of fighter planes, the pilots would give him "the works," going into steep dives or otherwise trying to rattle the older man. It never worked. As he did when he was a commander, "Slew" McCain earned the admiration of his subordinates with his toughness.[9]

He was also superstitious. He wore a nonregulation "ratty" green cap with an officer's insignia sewn into the visor. He believed the cap to be a lucky hat, and every sailor on his ships knew to take care of that hat—even when the wind threatened to blow it away. Many a sailor scrambled on the deck to retrieve that cap in the wind.[10]

"Slew" McCain first commanded land-based aircraft in the Pacific during World War II, and he was in charge during the crucial battle of Guadalcanal, in the Solomon Islands. The allies won that battle against the Japanese, but at a great cost in men and machinery. It also taught McCain about the need for superior air power, and he later became Deputy Chief of Naval operations for Air, the Navy's "air boss," as his grandson would put it in his autobiography.[11]

He returned to the Pacific to command the famous Carrier Task Force of the Third Fleet, which was credited with disabling and dismantling Japanese sea power, though also at great cost. His bravery never wavered, according to Navy records. Even when kamikaze Japanese planes attacked on their suicide missions, he stood fast, calmly expressing his belief that the guns on his ships would blast the planes out of the sky before they crashed into his ships. They did.[12]

When the war came to an end, Admiral William "Bull" Halsey, commander of the Pacific fleet and a close friend of McCain's, persuaded him to observe the Japanese surrender on the deck of the USS *Missouri*. McCain protested but eventually attended the surrender ceremony. He can be found in the famous pictures of the document signings, standing in the first row of Navy officers, on the left side, looking down. He later expressed gratitude that he had been there, but what he really wanted to do was get home.

He flew to San Diego after the September 2, 1945, surrender, arriving on September 6. His wife, Katherine Vaulx McCain, threw a welcome-home party for him the next day. In the middle of the celebration, he said he felt ill. He fell over and died.

His obituary was on the front page of the *New York Times* the next day. The story noted that McCain's air groups caught four Japanese convoys, sank 41 ships and damaged 28 more—believed to be a record for a one-day strike by fleet carriers.[13]

Eight years later, in July 1952, the destroyer USS *McCain* was launched at the Bath Iron Works in Bath, Maine. The Iron Works had distinguished itself in World War II by building ships at the rate of about one a week, and its ships were known worldwide for their quality and strength. The *McCain* was the longest ship ever built in Maine up to that time, and the tide on the Kennebec River had to be just right before the ship could be launched. Fleet Admiral Halsey, McCain's comrade and commander, gave a speech that day, extolling McCain as an "outstanding naval officer, a wonderful family man, a gentleman and my beloved comrade and friend. He gave all he had."[14]

He then choked up and could not continue, so emotional was the memory of his old friend.

Later that day, at a buffet luncheon for the family, Navy officials, and friends, Halsey encountered the 17-year-old "Johnny" McCain and asked if the young man drank. With some experience with alcohol behind him but warily eyeing his mother over his shoulder, McCain was obliged to say no. Halsey didn't hesitate. "Your grandfather drank bourbon and water," he said, summoning a waiter. "Bring the boy a bourbon and water."[15]

"Slew" McCain was profane, tough, superstitious, and strong. He rolled his own cigarettes and drank his share of liquor. He was small of stature but commanded his men with great resolve and respect. And, in return, they respected him. "Slew" passed on many of his traits to his grandson, John Sidney McCain III, not the least of which was that, for all of his fooling around, he took his job and his command very seriously.

"JACK"

John Sidney McCain Jr. was born in Council Bluffs, Iowa, but, as usual for the McCain family, that "hometown" was just another stop along the way, as his mother was visiting family there while his father was at sea. He grew up moving from town to town, as his family followed the Navy career of his father. When he was just 16, he went to the Naval Academy in Annapolis, a small (five-foot-six, a little over 100 pounds) youngster totally unprepared for the rigors that awaited him.[16]

He struggled at the Naval Academy, racking up demerits, getting barely passing grades, and getting in trouble more often than not. He came one demerit short of being dropped from the class, so he straightened up just enough to make it, graduating eighteenth from the bottom of the class. (Worse than his father, but better than his son would do!)[17]

Denied aviator status because he was found to be unqualified, "Jack" McCain decided to go into submarines. He would make his considerable reputation there, and his career did not suffer from its early fits and starts.

He commanded submarines in World War II in both the Atlantic and the Pacific and became famous in the Pacific theater as the commander of the USS *Gunnel*. On only the second of the *Gunnel's* patrols in the Pacific, the sub had a harrowing experience in which it sank a Japanese freighter and destroyer, was subjected to depth charges and efforts by a Japanese ship to grab onto it with fishing nets made of chains. The crew members were scared and praying. Then, the sub had to stay submerged for 36 hours with only short breaks, further endangering the crew because of lack of oxygen. The men not on duty were told to go to their bunks and lie down so that their bodies would use less air. The temperature in the sub was 120 degrees and the humidity was 100 percent. The crew would not last long under these conditions, particularly considering the lack of oxygen.

Eventually, McCain made a decision to surface and try to fight any Japanese ships that might be still looking for the sub. Another course of action, one he opposed but offered to his officers, was to abandon the ship and swim away, with a faint hope of rescue. To a man, they agreed with their skipper and rejected that course.[18]

Upon surfacing, the *Gunnel* found the Japanese destroyers steaming away. The danger passed, and the crew survived. Jack McCain received the Silver Star for the action.

Jack McCain was skillful as a sailor and an inspiration to his men. He had an ever-present cigar, and he also partied hard and drank, but never while on duty. At the end of the World War II, he joined his father in Tokyo Bay for the surrender, and the two met for the last time on the bridge of the submarine tender USS *Proteus*.

Jack McCain didn't make it home in time for his father's funeral, but the closeness he felt to his father stayed with him all of his life.

Jack McCain was truly was married to the Navy, but he also had an affection for women—particularly one.

Roberta Wright met Jack McCain when she was a 20-year-old junior at the University of Southern California, and Jack was stationed in Long Beach, California, while serving aboard the *Oklahoma* in 1931. She was the daughter of Archibald Wright, a rich oil man who had struck it big in Oklahoma and Texas and moved to California and essentially retired. He said he wanted to raise his daughters, Roberta, and her twin sister, Rowena.

The Wrights did not exactly approve of Roberta taking up with a sailor, so, when the two decided to get married, they eloped to Tijuana, Mexico, for a quickie marriage, on January 21, 1933, in Caesar's bar.[19]

The wedding got them both in trouble: Roberta with her parents and Jack with the Navy, which disciplined him for being away without leave, although not very severely (he was confined to the ship for 10 days with a stern warning for not having requested leave to get married).[20]

"He sure was a lot of fun," remembered Roberta McCain in an interview years later when Jack had been dead for many years and she was 96.[21]

She returned, married. Her skeptical family eventually accepted Jack McCain, probably because she would have it no other way.

Roberta McCain said that her mother, in particular, never understood the Navy, "I think she heard about a girl in every port. She thought it was just a terrible way to live," Roberta said.

The newly married McCains began the life of Navy families, moving around. For Roberta, it was the perfect life. She loved moving around and seeing new parts of the world. She traveled all her life and well into her 90s, usually with her sister as a traveling companion.

"Jack loved the Navy and he loved to go to work," Roberta McCain said. "He worked seven days a week if they needed him and it never bothered me."[22]

JOHN SIDNEY McCAIN III

John and Roberta McCain were stationed at Coco Solo, Panama, in what was then the U.S. Panama Canal Zone when John Sidney McCain III was born, the second of their three children, in the middle between sister Sandy and brother Joe. Roberta McCain recalled giving birth in a local Panamanian hospital on August 29, 1936, before air conditioning. In those days, fathers did not attend the birthing process but waited nearby for the good news. The windows of the hospital were open, and she could clearly hear the sounds of her husband celebrating the arrival of his first son with friends at a bar down the street.

She remembered it being swelteringly hot in Panama that summer, with her clothes sticking to her and insects everywhere. Yet she managed the task of birthing "Johnny" with aplomb.

"It was the only place we were ever stationed that I hated every day of it," she recalled. "It was just terrible. And not one of my friends had the loyalty to be pregnant at the same time—I was the only one," she said with a big, broad smile. "We had cotton dresses on and every one of them was sticking to me."[23]

It happened that both John McCain's father and grandfather were at the base at the time of his birth. A family photo shows the three of them together—all dressed in white—the admiral in dress uniform, his father in a white business suit, and "Johnny" in a christening gown.

John McCain's birthplace would cause some controversy in later years as some raised the issue of whether he could actually run for president since he was born not in the United States as required by the Constitution but in a territory controlled by the United States, the Panama Canal Zone. Historians and politicians eventually agreed that his birthplace was, in fact, United States soil, and the issue was dropped.

"Johnny" began the itinerant life of a Navy child. He has said that he lost track of how many schools he attended growing up, but it was somewhere around 20. He soon learned to cope in the best way he knew—with humor and with a certain tough side that dared schoolmates to cross him. "Johnny was a happy child," recalled Roberta McCain.[24] She didn't recall much of the tough stuff except to say that when "Johnny" flew into occasional rages, holding his breath and turning blue until he passed out, she was advised to dunk him into a bathtub filled with cold water. That usually stopped the tantrums.

He was a bright kid whose wisecracks sometimes got him in trouble. She recalled going to a christening of a ship with "Johnny" and sitting in the back seat of the car while Jack drove.

"I was brushing my hair in the back seat and he said some smart aleck thing. I cracked him in the back of the head," she recalled, with quick addendum that she was not often inclined to hit her children, with a hairbrush or anything else.[25]

He developed a tough skin and a gregarious personality, both traits that helped him move from school to school. "You had to be an athlete, a really good looker (John thinks he is) or you had to develop a good rap," recalled brother Joe McCain, who is six years younger. "He and I developed a good rap. John had the ability to tell a joke and get along. If you picked on him, he would either talk his way out or go at you with both fists."[26]

At St. Stephen's, a private school in the Washington, DC, area, teachers reported a defiant, unruly streak punctuated by those fists Joe talked about. But, after moving around the country to various schools, Roberta McCain decided her son needed stability, so he was enrolled at Episcopal High School in Alexandria, Virginia, a boarding school near where the family lived for a time.

Episcopal was where McCain began to find his strengths, despite the fact that he was still undisciplined, unruly, and quick to snap a flash of anger. Among other things, he found he liked sports, particularly wrestling, and that he loved history and literature. All three would remain with him all his life.

At Episcopal, he learned, slowly, to relax about being the "new kid." He would spend three years there and graduate from high school. Although he was branded "worst rat" in his first year there, an appellation that grew out of his racking up demerits and demonstrating a general lack of respect, he found some friends. A particular influence was William Ravenel, who was head of the English Department. Ravenel also coached the junior varsity football team and had served in General George Patton's tank corps during World War II; he still served in the reserves at the time of McCain's tenure at Episcopal High. Ravenel's conversance with all things military resonated with McCain, as well.

From Ravenel, McCain learned about Somerset Maugham, Shakespeare, sports, service, and life.

"He was one of the few people to whom I confided that I was bound for Annapolis and a Navy career," McCain recalled in 2008, during his second run for the presidency, "and to whom I confessed my reservations about my fate."[27]

Ravenel also instilled in McCain the Episcopal honor code: "I will not lie; I will not cheat; I will not steal; I will report the student who does." McCain reflected that he did not fully understand the things that Ravenel was talking about until he found himself in a Vietnamese prison many years later. When he got out of prison, he wanted to go to see Ravenel.

"He was the one guy I wanted to see when I got out of prison. . . . There wasn't anybody I felt I could talk to about it. I just wanted to see Ravenel. I wanted to tell him that I finally understood there in Hanoi what he had been trying to tell me all those years about life and what it means. I wanted to thank him and apologize for being so stupid."

He never got the chance. Ravenel collapsed and died of a massive heart attack in 1971. He was only 53. McCain didn't find out until he was released from prison two years later.[28]

As a wrestler, McCain wasn't the greatest, but he did hold the record for the "fastest pin" for two years—the record was broken in 1954. He wrestled in the 127-pound class in his senior year. He also played JV football and tennis.

His senior yearbook entry noted his nickname as the "Punk" and also noted that "his magnetic personality has won for him many life-long friends. But, as magnets must also repel, some have found him hard to get along with. John is remarkable for the amount of gray hair he has; this may come from his cramming for Annapolis or from his nocturnal perambulations."[29]

Ah, those "nocturnal perambulations!" McCain and his friends were infamous for taking off from Alexandria, Virginia, to go into nearby Washington, DC, and take in a burlesque show or two and try to pick up girls. Sometimes it worked, sometimes it didn't, but McCain and his buddies always told good stories about it in any case.

Edward Pritchard, who wrestled at Episcopal with McCain, said McCain was "quite a wrestler," whom he loved to watch in matches because what he lacked in finesse he made up in intensity. Pritchard said McCain wasn't a great student at Episcopal but did well in the subjects that interested him—history and literature.[30]

There was another incident at Episcopal that made an impression on the young McCain. In the fall of his senior year, a member of the JV football team had broken the training rules seriously enough to warrant his expulsion from the school. Ravenel called a team meeting at which the team member confessed his offense. Ravenel asked the team members to decide the player's fate. McCain, among others, noted that the player had not signed a document pledging to abide by the rules and had freely confessed his transgression.

McCain voted to keep him on the team. So did the others. Later, Ravenel told McCain he had made the right decision. Honor, it seemed, had sunk in.[31]

McCain graduated from Episcopal High School in 1954. Later that year, his father would drive him to Annapolis, Maryland, to the U.S. Naval Academy. Despite his rambunctious childhood, his academic ups and downs, his wildness, and his flouting of the rules, that was the place he always knew he would go. It would not be an entirely pleasant experience.

NOTES

1. President Franklin Delano Roosevelt, speech to Congress, December 8, 1941, Archives of the United States, http://www.archives.gov/education/lessons/day-of-infamy/.

2. John McCain with Mark Salter, *Faith of My Fathers* (New York: Random House, 1999), p. 79.

3. Ibid., pp. 18–21.

4. Ibid., p. 21.

5. John McCain, speech, McCain Field, Meridian, Mississippi, March 31, 2008, http://www.johnmccain.com/Informing/News/Speeches/4dd9f383-be1c-4c37-865a-c42421c8162b.htm.

6. Robert Timberg, *John McCain; An American Odyssey* (New York: Free Press, 1995), p. 22.

7. Paul Alexander, *Man of the People* (Hoboken, NJ: Wiley, 2003), p. 8.

8. McCain, *Faith of My Fathers*, p. 25.

9. Ibid.

10. Ibid., p. 15.

11. Ibid., p. 33.

12. Ibid., p. 36.

13. Associated Press, "Admiral J.S. M'Cain Dies on Coast at 61," *New York Times*, September 7, 1945, p. 1.

14. "More than 10,000 Persons Watch Launching of Destroyer Leader," *Bath Daily Times*, July 14, 1952, p. 3.

15. McCain, *Faith of My Fathers*, p. 46.

16. Ibid., p. 53.

17. Ibid., p. 62.

18. USS *Gunnel*, Second War Patrol, http://www.jmlavelle.com/gunnel/patrol2.htm.

19. Maureen Orth, "The Road Trip of 2 Lifetimes, and Still Going," *New York Times*, December 14, 2007, http://travel.nytimes.com/2007/12/14/travel/escapes/14sisters.html.

20. McCain, *Faith of My Fathers*, p. 50.

21. Roberta McCain, interview with author, Washington, DC, April 15, 2008.

22. Ibid.

23. Ibid.

24. Ibid.

25. Ibid.

26. Joseph McCain, interview with author, Washington, DC, April 11, 2008.

27. John McCain, speech at Episcopal High School, Alexandria, Virginia, April 1, 2008, http://www.johnmccain.com/Informing/News/Speeches/2a7b4a 33-8236-4c5c-841c-68611149570d.htm.

28. Timberg, *John McCain: An American Odyssey*, pp. 35–36.

29. Episcopal High School Web site, http://www.episcopalhighschool.org/about_ehs/media_inquiries/john_mccain_54/index.aspx.

30. Edward Pritchard, interview with author, Alexandria, Virginia, April 1, 2008.

31. John McCain, speech at Episcopal High School, Alexandria, Virginia, April 1, 2008.

Chapter 2

FIFTH FROM THE
BOTTOM: ANNAPOLIS

One weekend in 1955, in McCain's sophomore year at the Naval Academy, he went to lunch with friend and roommate Frank Gamboa. As usual in those days, young Filipino-enlisted men were the stewards in the mess hall. As the two ate, a first classman (a senior) began ordering the steward around unkindly, asking the waiter to bring him seconds.

"He [the first classman] started berating [the steward]," remembered Gamboa. "The guy was being a real jerk. John McCain leaned over and said, 'Why don't you stop picking on that guy, he's doing the best he can.'"

"The guy was startled to be confronted by a junior and said to John, 'What did you say?'"

"He's doing the best he can and you're giving him a hard time," McCain said.

"What's your name, mister?" the first classman said to McCain.

"John McCain. What's yours?"

Gamboa recalled that the first classman got "so flustered, he left the table. I was dumbfounded. Then McCain said, 'It really [upsets me] when I see someone with power lord it over a subordinate.'"

Gamboa had never seen anything like it. Such talking back to an upper classman was unheard of. But, then again, the academy had never seen or heard anything like John Sidney McCain III.[1]

But his presence there had been foreshadowed by the long legacies of his father and grandfather. His grandfather's portrait hung there prominently. His father was a captain at the time and was moving up in the Navy. The pressure on McCain to succeed was enormous.

Academically, he continued the trend he had started at Episcopal, doing well in the subjects he liked and just skating by in the courses he despised. There was a lot of mathematics and science at the Naval Academy then, and McCain would show up at a friend's room on the night before an exam, entreating his pal to teach him just enough to pass. He was a very quick learner, and classmates were amazed by his swift comprehension of even the most difficult courses. But he never put out more than was necessary to pass.

"I was adept at cramming for exams, and blessed with friends who did not seem to mind too much my requests for urgent tutorials, I managed to avoid complete disaster," McCain wrote. "I got by, just barely at times, but I got by."[2]

Outside academics, McCain was known as a real leader at the academy. Unfortunately, he tended to lead a rowdy crew. They were known as the "Bad Bunch," a self-imposed title that left no doubt that they were trying to get away with anything they could.

Mostly, getting away things meant partying and racking up demerits. McCain was sloppy in his appearance—shoes were never shined enough, belts were hanging, uniforms were torn and had holes. He also was the ringleader in small acts of disobedience, enough to get plenty of demerits but never enough to get him thrown out of the academy.

"The fundamental problem was I was very immature," McCain said. "I used that immaturity to excuse some of that behavior. I had not just grown up in the way perhaps I should have. So therefore, I set out to break every rule I could possibly break. As soon as I came close to the danger zone (enough demerits to be expelled) my performance improved radically. I wanted to break the rules, but I didn't want to get thrown out."[3]

In one incident, a group of midshipmen had squirreled away a television set in their dorm, which was against the rules. When they got caught, they agreed to decide who should take the responsibility by a "shake around" using the Rock, Paper, Scissors game—a tradition at the Naval Academy for deciding issues among midshipmen. When they discovered that if McCain lost, he would go over the 150-demerit limit and be expelled, the others agree to exclude him from the game. But he refused to drop out. Luckily, the "prize" landed on another classmate.[4]

There was another incident at the academy that illustrated McCain's toughness, willingness to take on authority, and penchant for skating close to the edge in behavior.

He did not get on very well with his company officer, a superior whom he chose to name "Ben Hart" in his autobiography, so as to protect the man from embarrassment at the stories he was about to tell about him.

Hart continually gave McCain "bad grease" grades—failing him in decorum, dress, the ability to keep his quarters neat, and so on. Combined with his lax academic performance, the "bad grease" grades kept him near or at the bottom of his class constantly.

One day, Hart had had enough of McCain's insolence and sloppiness. Hart went to McCain's quarters and turned his bedding upside down. Now, it might not have been the neatest in the dormitory, but at least it was made. McCain was outraged. Ignoring the entreaties of his roommates to ignore the event, McCain marched straight to Hart's office.

"Captain, please don't do that again. I am too busy to make my bed twice a day," McCain said before turning on his heel and stalking out. Hart didn't say a word, though he could have reprimanded McCain severely. It was just that way with John McCain, even as a lowly second-year midshipman.[5]

Despite that escape, McCain kept racking up demerits.

"By my reckoning, at the end of my second class year, I had marched enough extra duty to take me to Baltimore and back 17 times—which, if not a record, certainly ranks somewhere very near the top," McCain recalled in a speech at his alma mater in 2008.[6]

McCain and Gamboa seemed to be the most unlikely of companions. McCain, with Scotch-Irish forbearers, was steeped in three generations of Navy tradition. Gamboa was a first-generation American—both his parents were from Mexico. "He literally taught us the Navy culture," Gamboa remembered.[7] And Gamboa said McCain clearly didn't care about the disparity in their backgrounds; he chose Gamboa for his roommate.

Gamboa and several of McCain's other academy friends often went into Washington, where his parents were stationed during that time. Jack and Roberta McCain entertained them for hours with Navy tales, and Gamboa marveled over how John and his dad talked about history, the military, and government.

"He was, in my opinion, a most inspirational naval officer," Gamboa recalled. "His father had great pride in the U.S. Navy, and he could expound on any aspect of it. When we would go there for weekends, we would eventually end up in his study, and he would grill us on how we were doing in our studies."[8]

There was another aspect to the visits to Jack and Roberta McCain's Washington home that meant little to John McCain and Frank Gamboa at the time but foreshadowed things to come. Gamboa remembered that there were sometimes visiting congressmen at the house, and Jack McCain would introduce the young midshipmen as "the future leaders of the U.S. Navy in America."[9]

He was right about the leadership part, but he got the Navy part wrong. His son would later be a leader not in the Navy, but in the world that those old congressmen represented—politics.

McCain's time at the Naval Academy was an in-between one in American military history. The Korean War had ended in stalemate in 1953, and military events in Southeast Asia did not yet involve the United States. The country was enmeshed in fears over Communism, and there were "Red Scares" and allegations that some Americans had Communist, or "Red," leanings. There was fear that another shooting war might not be far away, particularly since the Soviet Union and Communist China were declared enemies.

France was involved in a war in Vietnam. France appealed for help from the United States, but President Dwight Eisenhower refused to send American troops while saying that defeat of Communists in Southeast Asia was very important to the United States. He and his aides were the first to voice the "domino theory" for Southeast Asia, looking at the countries there like dominos and suggesting that if one fell to the Communists, the rest would follow.

The French lost their war in Vietnam, and the country was divided into North and South Vietnam. Ho Chi Minh came to power in the North. These events figured into the background of John McCain's academy tenure.

While at the academy, McCain was well known as a ladies' man, and he also was quick with advice to his fellow midshipmen about how to handle women. Gamboa recalled him offering advice to the lovelorn, sort of the "Dear Abby" of academy mids. Gamboa said he once was trying to write a thank-you note to a young woman he had dated (a polite custom in those days). He was having a little trouble when McCain came along and grabbed the paper. Disgustedly, he threw it away, saying it was terrible. He asked Gamboa if he was interested in seeing the young woman again, and when he found out that he was, he proceeded to dictate a new letter, with much better prose.[10]

When it came to women, however, McCain had a story that topped them all. In June 1957, McCain sailed off on a cruise with some classmates. It was a "first-class" cruise, designed to teach the midshipmen something about life at sea that was experienced by enlisted men. Later that month, the ship docked in Rio de Janeiro for a nine-day port call.

A "port call" usually meant a round of parties, particularly in a place like Rio, famous for its nightclubs and beautiful women. McCain, by all accounts, took full advantage of all of it. He was getting ready to go back to his ship, tired from four days of partying, when he got talked into going to yet another party, where, he was told, he would be introduced to "a very beautiful girl."

Curiosity got the better of him, and he stuck around to meet the woman, who turned out to be not only beautiful but Brazil's most famous fashion model. By all accounts, he was completely blown away by this woman, whom he chose to call "Elena" in his memoir but whom his brother remembered as being named "Maria,"[11] which actually was her name, as she revealed half a century later in a newspaper interview when McCain was running for president in 2008. He was "loving and romantic," said Maria Gracinda Teixeira de Jesus.[12] At the time, she apparently was exquisite and smitten with McCain.

They spent a whirlwind five days together. When it was time for him to return to his ship, shipmates stood and cheered as the model drove up to the dock in her Mercedes sports car, and out leapt McCain.

He returned to Annapolis for just long enough to catch a return flight to Rio. They spent more time together, then corresponded regularly while he was back at the academy that fall. The Christmas issue of the *Log*, the academy's humor magazine, featured her picture and the caption "So Nice to Come Home To."

McCain made one last trip to Brazil to see her over Christmas, and reality began to set in for the couple. He could not give up his Navy career to go to Brazil permanently; she was not going to give up her lucrative modeling career. They parted and never saw each other again.

But there was one more contact. After McCain's graduation from the Naval Academy, in 1958, he received a telegram from Brazil: "Congratulations on your graduation. I'll always love you. Elena."[13]

McCain's graduation day was not memorable for him. President Eisenhower delivered the commencement address, but only the top 100 graduates got to shake his hand. The rest were introduced company by company and given their diplomas. McCain was anxious to get out of there and go on a trip to Europe with friends.

Thirty-five years later, McCain returned to a Naval Academy commencement, this time as the featured speaker.

"Thirty-five years ago I sat where you sit today, listening to my commander in chief, Dwight David Eisenhower," he said. "If one of my classmates had suggested then that I might someday enjoy the same privilege as President Eisenhower, I would have had very grave doubts about his suitability for future command," he said.[14]

But, all kidding aside, McCain took away great lessons from the academy—the importance of honor, courage, and devotion to his fellow man.

In his first step away from the academy, he was going to flight school, still years away from recognition of those values and what they would mean to him later.

NOTES

1. Frank Gamboa, interview with author, Fairfax, Virginia, April 2, 2008.

2. John McCain with Mark Salter, *Faith of My Fathers* (New York: Random House, 1999), p. 134.

3. John McCain, interview with author, Washington, DC, July 25, 2008.

4. Frank Gamboa, interview with author, Fairfax, Virginia, July 30, 2008 (e-mail).

5. McCain, *Faith of My Fathers*, p. 132.

6. John McCain, speech at the Naval Academy, Annapolis, Maryland., April 2, 2008, http://www.johnmccain.com/Informing/News/Speeches/9ab40f08-d2ce-46c4-bae4-18e65994927c.htm.

7. Frank Gamboa, telephone interview with author, Fairfax, Virginia, April 2, 2008.

8. Ibid.

9. Ibid.

10. Dan Nowicki and Bill Muller, "McCain Profile: Chapter 2: At the Naval Academy," *Arizona Republic*, March 1, 2007, http://www.azcentral.com/news/specials/mccain/articles/0301mccainbio-chapter2.html.

11. Joseph McCain, interview with author, Washington, DC, April 11, 2008.

12. Harold Emert and Patrick Sullivan, "Brazilian Beauty Recalls Hot Rio Affair with Young John McCain," *New York Daily News*, September 21, 2008, http://www.nydailynews.com/news/politics/2008/09/20/2008-09-20_brazilian_beauty_recalls_hot_rio_affair_.html.

13. Robert Timberg, *John McCain: An American Odyssey* (New York: Free Press, 1999), pp. 55–59.

14. Monica Norton, "Death Clouds Mids' Graduation; Accident Kills Colleague Hours before Ceremony," *Baltimore Sun*, May 27, 1993, p. 1B.

Chapter 3

BEFORE COMBAT

If anyone thought graduating from the Naval Academy would change John McCain, they were wrong. After graduation, he continued his wild ways—but now he had jet airplanes at his disposal.

He was assigned to flight school in Pensacola, Florida, which he treated as much as an ongoing party as he did a school for aviators. He spent much of his off-duty time at a bar called Trader John's, where aviators were entertained by local girls. He met a woman there whom he described as "Marie, the Flame of Florida" and took her to a party with some of his married flyer friends and their wives. "Marie" did not exactly fit in with the demure women at the party (she at one point cleaned her fingernails with a switchblade knife), but she did help McCain burnish his flamboyant reputation.[1]

McCain learned to fly at Pensacola, and, while he was not judged to be an expert at it, he did well enough. Pensacola was where he experienced the first of what was to be many plane crashes. He was practicing takeoffs and landings when he crashed his plane into Corpus Christi Bay. He was knocked unconscious by the crash and came to just as the plane was settling on the bottom. He cracked the canopy just enough to squeeze out and swim to the surface, where he was picked up and checked out. After a few x-rays, it was determined that he was not seriously injured.

He barely let the accident slow him down, let alone stop him, from continuing his partying. He took a few painkillers and was ready for "action" that evening. His father had decided to check on him, however, having heard about the accident, and sent another officer by to look in on him. When the officer knocked at his room, he found the place to be a disgusting mess but McCain in fine shape. He must have reported all of his findings to Jack McCain, since the entire officers quarters had to stand for inspection the following weekend.[2]

McCain deployed to the Mediterranean for a series of exercises in the early 1960s and found he enjoyed the seagoing part of his job. He liked being on a carrier and became adept at piloting the massive ships as well as flying airplanes.

One flight, however, became legendary when he flew too low over the Iberian Peninsula and took out some power lines. The tale eventually grew to the point where it was said that McCain "turned the lights out in Spain."[3]

In addition to giving him freedom to enjoy his partying, being a bachelor gave McCain the opportunity to spend some of his free leave time attending "escape and evasion" school to prepare for the possibility of being shot down. Most of the training consisted of exercises in escape and evasion, to keep from falling into the hands of the enemy after being shot down. McCain was one of only two members of the team to avoid "capture" after five days in the Black Forest in Germany and to return to the specified rendezvous spot. He was provided only the amount of equipment that an ordinary pilot would have, a flight suit and a few "C" rations—canned food normally allotted to pilots during combat. Because he avoided capture during that exercise (and two others), he was not subjected to the mock interrogations that some of the others were put through. He did, however, have the opportunity to talk to an Air Force major who had been a prisoner of war in Korea and found remarkable the major's ability to deal with having been kept in solitary confinement.[4]

In October 1962, McCain was returning to home port at Norfolk after completing one of the Mediterranean deployments aboard the carrier *Enterprise* when suddenly he was told to fly his airplane back to the carrier. He and the other pilots were told there was a hurricane on the way (which did not match the weather reports they had heard). Some planes that attempted to land on the carrier were unable to and were told to return to base. The pilots were very curious about what was really going on. Soon, they found out.

President John F. Kennedy's speech confirming that the Soviets had placed nuclear missiles in Cuba—just 90 miles off the coast of Florida— was piped into the *Enterprise*. The Cuban missile crisis, as it came to be known, was under way. The crisis would severely test the Kennedy presidency and would fill the entire nation with dread about the real possibility of a nuclear war that could kill millions of Americans. As McCain and the other men on the *Enterprise* crowded around the speakers to listen, Kennedy spoke:

> Within the past week, unmistakable evidence has established the fact that a series of offensive missile sites is now in preparation on that imprisoned [Cuban] island. The purpose of these bases can be none other than to provide a nuclear strike capability against the Western Hemisphere.
>
> This urgent transformation of Cuba into an important strategic base—by the presence of these large, long-range, and clearly offensive weapons of sudden mass destruction—constitutes an explicit threat to the peace and security of all the Americas. . . .
>
> Our goal is not the victory of might, but the vindication of right; not peace at the expense of freedom, but both peace and freedom, here in this hemisphere, and, we hope, around the world. God willing, that goal will be achieved.[5]

There was no doubt that the *Enterprise* aircraft carrier and its crew was part of the "might" Kennedy was contemplating to achieve that victory.

As John McCain's 2008 presidential campaign described his retelling of the story:

> The *Enterprise,* sailing at full speed under nuclear power, was the first carrier to reach the waters off Cuba. For about five days, we believed we were going into action. We had never been in combat before, and despite the global confrontation a strike on Cuba portended, we were prepared and anxious to fly our first combat mission. Flyers and crewmen alike adopted a cool-headed, business-as-usual attitude toward our mission, but inwardly we were as excited as we could be.[6]

Fortunately, their military acumen was not needed. Following the speech and a blockade of Cuba by American ships, the Soviets decided to dismantle the nuclear weapons several days later, in return for which the United States agreed not to invade the island nation, and the worst nuclear crisis the United States had ever faced passed without a shot being fired.[7]

For McCain and his flying compatriots, emotions were running high. While none of them would admit to wanting war, their "appetites were whetted and our imaginations fueled."[8]

"But I had also begun to recognize that military service and war were more than an adventure for boys with vivid imaginations and a measure of audacity," he said years later. "They offered admission into history, possibly a big part of history, a much more daunting enterprise than proving one's mettle and with much greater things at stake than personal reputation or even the life and death of soldiers. The Cuban missile crisis could have caused a nuclear war, and we had been part of our country's response to the threat, but used in such a way to help forestall a chain of events from running to that terrible conclusion."[9]

In his personal life, McCain hadn't exactly settled down by then, but he was taking the Navy more seriously, and he was beginning to believe there might be an end to all the debauchery. By 1964, he was back at Pensacola, Florida. Also that year, he began a romance with Carol Shepp, the divorced mother of two boys. Shepp had dated and eventually married a classmate of McCain's at Annapolis, but that marriage had dissolved. She and McCain met again while she was visiting another friend. A romance blossomed. McCain found himself flying often to Philadelphia, where Carol lived with her two boys, Andy and Doug.

"I didn't think he'd ever get married," said John's brother, Joe McCain. Joe had been witness to John's series of beautiful women, each more exotic than the last, it seemed, and looked at John as living the epitome of the bachelor's life. "John had a revolving door policy for women, and they were uniformly attractive."[10]

But Carol appeared to be special. She was attractive, a former model, and fun-loving, as well.

McCain was transferred in 1964 to Meridian, Mississippi, to the Naval Air Station known as "McCain Field," named for his grandfather. He was a flight instructor there and flew three times a day himself, honing his pilot's skills. He also flew up to see Carol often, sometimes taking a student pilot along for training.

Meanwhile, his personal lifestyle craziness continued in Meridian. The base had decided to try to beautify the place by creating artificial lakes. However, they mostly looked like swamps, with mosquitoes to spare. One Navy wag named the pond "Lake Fester," and McCain and a group of his buddies built a makeshift "club" on a tiny island in the middle of the lake, dubbing it the "Key Fess Yacht Club." Parties there were legendary, and the reputation of the "Yacht Club" spread throughout the Navy.

But McCain was spending less and less of his time there as his relationship with Carol Shepp grew. And there was the possibility that he was settling down, just a bit, as his relationship deepened and the specter of going to fight in the war in Vietnam loomed in his future. In Vietnam,

1965 saw the beginning of operation "Rolling Thunder," a three-year air bombardment campaign by the United States against North Vietnam in which McCain and his fellow pilots would soon play a large role.

John McCain and Carol Shepp were married July 3, 1965. It was a small family wedding, and the reception was held at the famous Bookbinder's Restaurant in Philadelphia, which was owned by the family of Carol's college roommate, Connie Bookbinder. John and Carol made an attractive couple.

"I remember John and dad in dress whites at the wedding," recalled Joe McCain.[11]

McCain was still stationed at Meridian during the early years of his marriage to Carol, and he made the shift from wild bachelor to slightly more subdued family man rather easily. He had adopted Carol's two sons, and the couple fell into a group of young Navy couples and their friends and became regulars on the dinner party circuit. They worked hard, and they played hard, too, but the parties had a somewhat different cast to them than the bachelor debauchery.

"We were all young," said Naomi Belisle somewhat wistfully, 40 years later. Jerry Belisle was also an instructor and a Navy aviator who had known McCain before and after his marriage. "We had dinner parties, hors d'oeuvres and drinks and drinks with a meal and after-dinner drinks," she said. "That was our party. Nobody got falling down drunk. We were parents and we had responsibilities, and our guys flew jets."[12]

There was wonderful camaraderie among the Navy families, in part because they never knew when they would have to leave, be reassigned, or have their men go into combat.

Lewis and Morele Rosenfeld owned a women's clothing store in Meridian but had become friendly with the Belisles through their synagogue, and they were welcomed into the group of Navy men and their wives. They soon became good friends with the McCains, as well.

"I knew John before he ever married Carol," Morele Rosenfeld remembered. "He was in his late twenties. I thought he was cute as the devil."

But she was also "very fond of John and Carol" as a couple. Rosenfeld remembered that when they would go to the McCains' home, they would find their wedding pictures not in the living room or dining room but in the bathroom. That was because, according to Carol, "when John's buddies would fly through, they wouldn't go through the pictures on the coffee table, they would see them in the bathroom and then they would believe that they were married," Rosenfeld remembered.[13]

It was because of the Rosenfeld's women's store, Kay's Inc., that McCain discovered another talent—that of fashion show narrator. The Navy

wives decided to put on a charity fashion show, modeling some of the
clothes from the store, with Rosenfeld describing the frocks.

Shortly, here came McCain who decided to take over the narrating du-
ties, in a decidedly more irreverent way. "John didn't know a pair of pants
from a skirt," Rosenfeld laughed, "but he started narrating, and he was a
hoot. The next year, everyone said, 'You've got to get McCain.' By then
he had transferred back to Pensacola, but he came back and did another
show."[14]

In December 1965, McCain flew to Philadelphia, alone, to go to an
Army-Navy football game with his parents. His mother gave him a bunch
of Christmas gifts for Carol and the kids to take back to Meridian with
him. As he flew close to Norfolk, Virginia, to refuel on the return trip, his
engine flamed out. He tried three times to go through the procedures to
restart the engine, but they failed, and he was forced, again, to eject from
his airplane. It was a "routine" ejection and he was unscathed. The gifts,
however, were lost.

On September 2, 1966, Carol gave birth to Sidney Ann, their daughter, and shortly thereafter McCain was transferred to Jacksonville, where
he joined a squadron scheduled to go to Vietnam.

It was a routine posting for a Navy aviator, and one that McCain had
been pointing toward all of his career. In mid-1967, he was deployed to
the aircraft carrier USS *Forrestal*, the largest in the Navy. With her husband at sea, Carol decided to take the kids and move to London, where
Jack and Roberta McCain were stationed.

McCain's assignment to the *Forrestal* would be anything but routine.

NOTES

1. John McCain with Mark Salter, *Faith of My Fathers* (New York: Random
House, 1999), p. 154.

2. Robert Timberg, *John McCain: An American Odyssey* (New York: Free
Press, 1999), pp. 70–71.

3. Ibid., p. 73.

4. McCain, *Faith of My Fathers*, p. 159.

5. President John F. Kennedy, Cuban missile crisis address to the nation,
Oct. 22, 1962, http://www.americanrhetoric.com/speeches/jfkcubanmissilecrisis.
html.

6. John McCain, campaign "Service to America Tour" speech, April 2, 2008,
Pensacola, Florida, http://www.johnmccain.com/Informing/News/Speeches/f4e9
442b-18fa-489c-8255-9d323db42542.htm.

7. Global Security.org, Cuban Missile Crisis history, http://www.globalsecu
rity.org/military/ops/cuba-62.htm.

8. McCain, *Faith of My Fathers*, p. 161.

9. John McCain, campaign "Service to America Tour" speech, April 2, 2008, Pensacola, Florida.

10. Joseph McCain, interview with author, Washington, DC, April 11, 2008.

11. Ibid.

12. Naomi Belisle, telephone interview with author, Baton Rouge, Louisiana, July 26, 2008.

13. Morele Rosenfeld, telephone interview with author, Meridian, Mississippi, July 26, 2008.

14. Ibid.

Chapter 4

VIETNAM: INTERCEPTING A SAM

I'm not a hero, I intercepted a surface-to-air missile with my own airplane.

—*John McCain, joking while campaigning for president, 2000*

July 29, 1967, looked to be like an ordinary day of war on the USS *Forrestal*. A-4 aircraft were lined up on the flight deck, ready for takeoff on missions over North Vietnam. John McCain already had flown five bombing runs over Vietnam—this would be the sixth for the 31-year-old pilot—and everything appeared routine.

He was third in line on the port (left) side of the ship. Suddenly, a Zuni missile flew directly at him, hitting the fuel tank of his A-4 Skyhawk. Jet fuel spilled everywhere and became a rolling fireball. The Zuni, it was later proven, was launched because of a stray electrical short. It was an accident—the worst on an aircraft carrier since World War II.

"Fahr, fahr, fahr—fahr on the flight deck, fahr on the flight deck! All hands, man your battle stations," came the voice over the ship's intercom, with a vaguely southern accent.

McCain popped the canopy on his aircraft, scrambled out, and crawled on his hands and knees out over the nose and along the long probe used for refueling. Fire was everywhere. But he had to get off that airplane before the bombs it was carrying blew up. He had no choice. He jumped into the flames and started running away from the raging jet-fuel fire, slapping at flames sprouting on his flight suit. He had taken just a few steps when a bomb exploded from the fire and heat—"cooked off," in sailor's parlance, to describe a bomb detonated by heat, not impact.

McCain was hit by shards of shrapnel but not seriously injured. He made his way to the sick bay of the ship, dodging the fire and exploding bombs on deck.

The scene in sick bay was worse, if that's possible, than the inferno on the deck. Everywhere, men lay dying, most of them horribly burned. Many severe burn victims do not die instantly, but their fate is nonetheless sealed. Some can talk, at least for a while. McCain remembered that one young sailor asked him about the fate of a fellow pilot. Assured the pilot was okay, the sailor murmured, "Thank, God," and died.[1]

Returning to the deck, McCain feared that the ship might be lost. But the sailors valiantly fought the fire, aided by some other ships which pulled alongside and sprayed water and saved the Forrestal.

But the ship was in wretched condition. It left the combat zone and headed for the Subic Bay naval base in the Philippines. There were 134 sailors dead, and the rest were wounded or stunned. The largest carrier in the fleet was crippled, her crew exhausted and haunted. Twenty-six airplanes were destroyed, including 14 A-4 attack bombers like McCain's and nine F-4B Phantom fighters, along with three reconnaissance planes. Thirty-one aircraft were damaged, at least four of which would have to be scrapped, and about 12 others were not flyable.[2]

Among the dead were many aircraft technicians, the men who maintained the aircraft and readied them for flight. And dozens of sailors who had gone to sleep in their berths several decks below the flight deck were killed by the intense fire and heat, probably before they ever knew what hit them. Others died as heroes, hauling fire hoses toward the flames even as bombs were going off in every direction. Some said the fire was so intense that it essentially vaporized some of the sailors on the deck.

"I don't think the men of the Forrestal could have reacted better," Chief Aviation Ordnanceman Thomas Lawler told the Navy magazine All Hands for its November 1967 issue. "I think the training they had been given really showed up then, although you can't really train for any given situation. You can train a man to fight a fire, but you can't train him to go in blindfolded and fight a fire in the face of exploding ordnance. There has to be some devotion to duty involved, too."[3]

Their reactions to the disaster were good, their shock at the aftermath evident. But there was another emotion, mostly unspoken in the face of death—disappointment. The Forrestal had been on the way to engage in sustained combat off the coast of North Vietnam. Now, that would have to wait. It was not unlike the letdown after the Cuban missile crisis—the crew members, particularly pilots, would never say they wanted war. But they were trained for it, ready for it, and anxious to use their skills.

McCain, shocked and subdued, didn't really know what he was going to do next. So, he took advantage of an unusual opportunity. A *New York Times* reporter who was covering the war in Vietnam rode a helicopter out to the *Forrestal* to do the story in the wake of the accident. The reporter, R. W. "Johnny" Apple, who would make a name for himself with his Vietnam War coverage, interviewed McCain for his newspaper article, and the two found they liked each other. Apple offered McCain a ride to Saigon, the capital of South Vietnam, for a little respite. "R and R," they called it in the service, rest and relaxation. The gregarious Apple was an expert at food and drink, as well as wartime coverage, and McCain took him up on the offer.

That the two hung around together for a few days in Saigon after the *Forrestal* fire was not widely known at the time. But later, in recalling that time, Apple wrote that McCain, shaken by the fire and the bombs going off, questioned his resolve as a bomber pilot.

"It's a difficult thing to say," Apple quoted McCain as observing. "But now that I've seen what the bombs and the napalm did to the people on our ship, I'm not so sure that I want to drop any more of that stuff on North Vietnam."[4]

But a big part of McCain was still anxious to get back into the fight. Before he had left on his R and R with Apple, an officer from the carrier USS *Oriskany* had appeared on the crippled *Forrestal* to ask if any pilots would like to transfer to his ship, which had lost a number of pilots. McCain and some others signed up.

He had a few weeks break before the *Oriskany* was to leave port for Vietnam, so he flew to Europe, where Carol and the kids had gone to stay. They were near London, England, where Jack McCain was serving as Commander-in-Chief, United States Naval Forces, Europe. He spent a pleasant few weeks with them. His orders for the *Oriskany*, however, were delayed, so he and the family went back to the Jacksonville, Florida, area, where he rented a house for his family. Then he joined the *Oriskany*, expecting to be back in Florida in about a year.

In 1967, the United States had escalated the bombing over North Vietnam, particularly Hanoi, in an effort to counteract the North Vietnamese war machine. The targets were carefully selected, however, as members of the U.S. government did not want to strike targets that might be used for propaganda purposes—schools or hospitals, for example.

The problem was that many people in the United States were beginning to turn against the war, not those in the military like McCain, but many others, led by young people, particularly those on college campuses. There was a draft for military service during that time—all men 18 and over had to register—and every male knew that he was in line to be drafted. Women did not have to register. But a series of "deferments," special categories, could postpone (sometimes indefinitely) military service. Staying in college or graduate school was one way to get a deferment, so young men who could afford it went to college. Getting married was another option, as was failing the induction physical. Getting too fat or too thin was a popular way to fail, if difficult to maintain. And some young men, determined to avoid the war, fled to Canada or other countries where they hid as fugitives.

This was not the culture of the U.S. Navy, where McCain served, but it was very much a part of the country, which was divided over the war. President Lyndon Johnson, who had succeeded John F. Kennedy as president after Kennedy was assassinated, on November 22, 1963, found himself pressed to escalate the war in Vietnam. His advisers were saying that an escalation might break the will of the North Vietnamese and lead, eventually, to a U.S. victory. Johnson chose that path, but he knew that much of the country and the electorate that he would be facing in 1968 was opposed. Thus, the targets for the so-called Rolling Thunder bombing campaign were chosen very carefully. Johnson himself picked some of the targets while sitting in the White House.[5]

On October 22, 1967, one of the largest protests in American history concentrated on Washington, DC—a massive antiwar rally surrounding the Pentagon. But the war kept going.

Just four days after the antiwar demonstration, John McCain climbed into his A-4 Skyhawk for his twenty-third bombing mission. His target that day was a solid one—the power plant in Hanoi, the heavily defended capital of North Vietnam. There was no quarrel with this target; it was an important one, worth the risk of dodging Soviet-made surface-to-air (SAM) missiles that would be aimed at him while he attempted to achieve his mission.

The flak, or anti-aircraft fire, was very thick that day. The Skyhawk bombers had three separate warning devices to indicate that enemy SAMs were approaching—a flashing light and one tone sounded when a missile's radar was tracking the plane, another when it had locked onto the plane, and a third indicating that a SAM was headed for the plane. McCain and other pilots described a SAM as looking like a flying telephone pole. There were lots of "telephone poles" in the sky.

McCain found his target and dove toward it just as the tone went off signaling him that a SAM was headed for his plane. He could have broken off the attack and used evasive maneuvers to get out of the way of the missile, but he made the decision to stay on course and drop his bombs, then try to execute the "jinking" evasive maneuvers. But just as the bombs left his aircraft, the surface-to-air missile slammed into his plane. Before he could think, he was plummeting down into enemy territory.[6]

NOTES

1. John McCain with Mark Salter, *Faith of My Fathers* (New York: Random House, 1999), p. 179.

2. R. W. Apple Jr., "The *Forrestal* Toll May Reach 125; 69 Still Missing," *New York Times*, July 31, 1967, p. 1.

3. "A Ship Full of Heroes," *All Hands*, November 1967, p. 11.

4. R. W. Apple Jr., "Adm. McCain's Son, *Forrestal* Survivor, Is Missing in Raid," *New York Times*, October 28, 1967, p. 1.

5. Lt. Col. Michael W. Kometer, USAF, "Command in Air War: Centralized vs. Decentralized control of Combat Air Power," Ph.D. dissertation, Massachusetts Institute of Technology, May 2005, http://esd.mit.edu/people/dissertations/kometer_michael.pdf.

6. McCain, *Faith of My Fathers*, p. 188.

Chapter 5

PRISONER

McCain reached up and pulled the ejection seat handle, blasting him into the Vietnamese sky. He hit part of the airplane on the way out, breaking his left arm, his right arm in three places, and his right knee, which probably hit the instrument panel. His parachute opened, but just barely before he hit, and he plunged into Truc Bach Lake, a small body of water in the middle of downtown Hanoi, the capital of North Vietnam.[1]

He hit the bottom of the lake, pushed off with his good leg, and broke the surface. But, wearing 50 pounds of flight gear, he sank right back down again. He broke the surface a second time but couldn't figure out why he couldn't lift his arms to inflate his life vest. Finally, he grabbed the vest toggles with his teeth and bobbed to the surface. His problems had just begun.

He had landed in the middle of the most heavily fortified city in the middle of the day. As he ruefully put it, "Escape would have been challenging."[2]

There was to be no escape. He was immediately surrounded by an angry mob of Vietnamese citizens. He had, of course, been dropping bombs on their city, and they were understandably upset. The gang dragged him out of the lake and began beating him in various places, including the limbs that were already horribly injured. One woman stopped the mob. She tied up his wounds and then held a cup of tea to his lips while another took pictures—for propaganda purposes, probably.

One man who was involved in the episode was Mai Van On, a storeroom clerk at the Minister of Industry. On had left work and gone to a bomb shelter when he saw McCain's plane fall out of the sky. He ran to the lake and jumped in to save McCain. Fighting off shouts from other Vietnamese, On pulled McCain out of the lake.[3]

"About 40 people were standing there. They were about to rush him with their fists and stones. I asked them not to kill him. He was beaten for a while before I could stop them," On said in an interview 33 years later.[4]

By then, his injuries were beginning to sink in, and McCain saw that his leg was twisted at right angles, in an unnatural direction. He cried out, "My God, my leg!" but that seemed to make the crowd even angrier. McCain finally was loaded onto a truck and driven to a prison, Hoa Lo, in the center of the city. Prisoners had named the prison the "Hanoi Hilton."

"No American reached Hoa Lo in worse physical condition than McCain," wrote John Hubbell in his book about the Vietnam prisoner of war experience, *P.O.W.*[5]

For several days, McCain was virtually unattended except for a bit of water and food the attendants would bring him. He drifted in and out of consciousness, but he spent more and more time not conscious. Several days later, he got a look at his leg. His knee was swollen to the size, shape—and color—of a football. He panicked, remembering a fellow aviator who had slammed a leg upon ejection from a plane, and, when the blood pooled in the leg, he had died. McCain pleaded with his captors to take him to a hospital. They refused, apparently believing that he was going to die.[6]

Suddenly, things changed. A Vietnamese interrogator the prisoners called "The Bug" burst into the room. "Your father is a big admiral! Now we will take you to the hospital!"[7]

The Vietnamese had figured out who McCain was. That fact probably saved his life again. He was taken to a hospital, put in a relatively clean bed (though the place was generally filthy), and given blood and plasma.

Half a world away, Jack and Roberta McCain were in London, getting ready to go to a party at the Iranian ambassador's residence, when a special telephone given to the high-ranking Navy officials, rang.

"I never touched the thing," Roberta McCain remembered. "But Jack was in the shower and we were in a hurry, so I answered it. It was Rear Admiral Hank Miller. And he said, 'Roberta, two planes were shot down, one of them was Johnny's, but we saw no ejections.' When Jack came out of the shower, [I told him and] we decided to go on to the dinner party and not to say anything."[8]

After the party, Roberta and Jack were home when the phone rang again. This time, it was Chief of Naval operations Tom Moorer, who said the same thing, that they didn't believe anyone had survived the crash. Roberta called Carol, back in Jacksonville, who already had been contacted by the Navy.

"And I said I think Johnny's really dead, don't you? And she said 'yes.' And I said, 'Well, we're going to make our plans,'" Roberta remembered.[9]

Joe McCain was working for a newspaper in San Diego that fall. He was awakened in the middle of the night to find both his mother and his father on the telephone from London, a highly unusual event.

"They said they had some news. Johnny's been shot down over Hanoi. I just remember feeling like one of those wrecking balls you see in the movies pausing a bit because the next question in my mind was, well, what happened. They said we understand he didn't make it. That's when that wrecking ball hit me right in the middle of the chest," Joe McCain said.

"I said, 'What do we do now?' I remember my father saying, 'We just really need to pray for the boy.'"[10]

Prayer would have been appropriate.

Two days later, the *New York Times* reported that "Admiral McCain's Son, *Forrestal* Survivor, Is Missing in Raid." It was the story by Johnny Apple that recounted their time together after the *Forrestal* fire. Although McCain's status was still unknown, the story had some characteristics of an obituary, listing details of McCain's family background and his career at the Naval Academy. But a later article confirmed that he had been "captured."[11]

Joe McCain was jolted awake the next morning by his clock radio in San Diego, which was tuned to the all-news station XTRA, broadcasting out of Mexico. The radio reported "this thing about an admiral's son having been captured. And I woke up saying, 'They even named him!'" Joe McCain remembered. Several people came up to him that day with long faces saying how sorry they were that his brother had been captured, but he was happy, rather than sad. Two days ago, he had thought his brother was gone for good.[12]

Roberta McCain was in Europe, looking after her daughter Sandy's three children. They were visiting a country house, and all of a sudden, the stewards "came flying out of the house shouting, 'Johnny was shot down, he's a prisoner, he's a prisoner of war.' Can you believe that was the best news I ever heard in my life? It depends on where you're at, you see," she said.[13]

After McCain had spent a few days in the North Vietnamese hospital, doctors tried to "set" McCain's right arm, which was broken in three places. It was tricky, and it wouldn't go together. After three hours of trying, without anesthetic, the doctors gave up and just slapped a plaster cast on it. McCain was in excruciating pain.

They moved him into a cleaner room and a bed with white sheets. That's when he first met the North Vietnamese man who came to be known as "The Cat." He was the commander of all the prison camps, but

McCain did not know that at the time. The Cat told him that a French journalist wanted to see him and film him.

Through his delirium, McCain said he wasn't sure he wanted to be filmed. No matter, he was going to be interviewed anyway. The North Vietnamese were not about to let the opportunity pass for "The Prince," as they called McCain, to be filmed for propaganda.

The Cat said that unless McCain cooperated with the reporter and said that he was sorry for his crimes and that he was being well treated, he would not be given the two operations he needed on his knee. McCain consented to the interview, but, even in severe pain, he was calculating exactly what he would say. What he didn't count on was that the reporter would be sympathetic, after a fashion, to his plight.

The French TV crew was led by Francois Chalais. The film, which later became famous in "McCain for President" television ads, shows McCain lying in the bed, smoking a cigarette, his broken arm held up by the cast. His eyes look filmy—even his mother thought they had drugged her son. But it was simply the result of severe pain.

The Cat told McCain that he had to tell the interviewer that his treatment was humane and lenient. McCain didn't say he would do that but apparently satisfied the Cat enough that he let the interview go on.

Chalais and his crew were let into the room. McCain said his treatment had been satisfactory and that doctors had promised to operate on his leg. Off camera, the Cat was visibly upset and told McCain he had to say that his treatment was humane. McCain refused, but then Chalais broke in to say what McCain had said was enough. On the film, McCain told Carol and the children that he was getting better and that he loved them. When the Cat and others asked him to call for an end to the war, McCain would not, and, again, Chalais said he had enough on that subject.

"How is the food?" Chalais asked.

"Well, it's not Paris, but I eat it," McCain replied.[14]

Jack and Roberta McCain were told about the video, and they wanted to see it. Jack got the call from the French newsman telling him to fly from London to Paris to view the film. They were about to go, but a snowstorm closed the airport. By the time they got back home, *Time* magazine had heard about the film and wanted to interview Jack about it, Roberta said, even before he had seen it.

They finally viewed the film. As a mother, it was tough to take, Roberta recalled, but she thought her son had been drugged (she found out the truth years later) and was just grateful he was alive, albeit in terrible condition.

"You just kind of go dense," she said. "I'm pretty stoic. I accept things. I don't believe in fantasy or fooling yourself."[15]

IN PRISON

There were no fantasies in Hanoi. McCain was in terrible shape and unable to do anything for himself. The North Vietnamese did eventually operate on the mangled leg, but rather crudely. He was not getting any better; in fact, he was getting worse. He still had fevers; his infections went untreated. He could neither stand nor walk and was having extreme trouble keeping food and water down. His weight dropped below 100 pounds. He was wasting away.

McCain asked to be put with other Americans. For some reason—speculation suggests that it might have been because they didn't want to be responsible if he died—the North Vietnamese complied. They took McCain to another prison, called by prisoners "The Plantation," outside Hanoi. There, he had the sweet good fortune to be shoved into a cell with Air Force Colonel George "Bud" Day and Norris Overly, an Air Force major. The two did nothing less than nurse him back to life.[16]

Day was a story in himself. He had been shot down on August 26, 1967, north of Vietnam's "Demilitarized Zone," or DMZ, which separated North Vietnam from South Vietnam. He, too, had mangled a leg ejecting from his F-100 fighter jet airplane and had broken his right arm in three places. He was captured and his fractured limbs roughly set, and then he was put into a hole in the ground until he could be transported north. Day, however, had other ideas.

He waited until it was dark, slipped his ropes, and decided to try to walk to the other side of the DMZ, where there was an American base, 20 miles away. It would have been a daunting trek for a healthy soldier. But he was badly injured and sick. He had no food; he existed on dew and berries and an occasional frog he caught—which promptly made him sicker.

He walked in circles sometimes and traveled at night so as not to be recaptured. He barely evaded the enemy several times. Thirteen days later, he found himself within sight of the American base. He could hear helicopters landing and taking off. It was nighttime and he faced a decision—run for it, sprinting across what was probably a field full of landmines and risk being shot by his own countrymen who might not guess that the haggard, ragged, limping man was one of their own, or wait until dawn. Another man might have been so overcome by the proximity of safety that he would have run for it. Bud Day decided to wait.

It appeared to be the right decision. But it turned out very badly. In the morning, only several yards from the base, he was spotted by two North Vietnamese soldiers. They shouted at him to stop; he didn't. They shot him in the leg. He fell to the ground and hid as best he could, but they found him. They tortured him on the way back to Hanoi. Bud Day would have to wait another six years for his freedom.[17]

"As unfortunate as his capture was for Bud, it was salvation for many others. Few leaders in Vietnam's prisoner-of-war camps were as honorable, brave, and inspiring as he was. Included in the credit he can always claim is my life," McCain wrote in *Hard Call: the Art of Great Decisions*.[18]

The McCain that Day and Overly saw when he was put into their cell was just shy of dead.

"He was in a huge body cast, right arm sticking out of that cast like a stick out of a snowman," Day said. "His right knee was mangled, his left arm was dislocated and hanging out of his socket. He was about 97 pounds and his eyes were fever bright. I was certain he was going to die before morning. My sense was that the Vietnamese had dumped him off on me to make it appear that Americans had neglected him to death. But John had no intention of dying."[19]

McCain was so excited to see other Americans that he talked constantly and wanted to know everything they knew about other prisoners and what life was like at the Plantation. He talked that first night until he fell asleep, no matter that he was still in horrible condition. Little by little, Overly and Day washed him, assisted him in relieving himself, helped him eat a little, and made him healthier.

He got so he could stand up, then walk a little on crutches. He was eating better, too, and the food had improved a bit. McCain and the others were unsure why they were getting slightly better treatment. They weren't in the dark long. It turned out that the North Vietnamese were getting ready to release a few prisoners, including Overly, as part of an "amnesty" grant. Overly told Day and McCain of the offer, and both said he should reject it because the military code of conduct required that prisoners be released in the order they were captured—longest held captive, first released. But Overly decided to go another way and take early release.

Many in the prison resented Overly for his decision. But McCain owed him his life and therefore was put into a difficult position. He accepted Overly's decision with equanimity, and Overly left the prison with a letter from McCain to Carol in his pocket.[20]

McCain's decision not to hold a grudge against Overly was reflective of his attitude about many things. It could be summed up as: Experience it, process it, and move on. McCain did not dwell on misfortune, nor did he try to relive the past or think what might have been. He dealt with reality as it existed, tried to do as best he could within that reality. It was not that he forgot the past—hardly. But he somehow seemed to be able to remember, even under the most horrible of circumstances, to put those things behind him.

After Overly's departure, McCain got stronger. That was a blessing and a curse, as his captors decided he was now strong enough to live on his own—in solitary confinement. He would be in solitary for two years.

Two years! Seven hundred and thirty days; 730 sunrises; 730 sunsets; perhaps two "meals" a day, rare walks outside his 10-by-10-foot cell. He could see the courtyard from a slit in his door, and he would often shout insults to his captors, using the insolence that had sustained him at the Naval Academy and elsewhere growing up. That small act of defiance may have helped him cope with the situation.

Men who are deprived of company often retreat into fantasy. McCain did some of that, but he also relied on the practical to keep his mind sharp. He tried to remember the names of everyone in the prison camp; he recited what he could recall of movies and books, he memorized all the men in his squadron, their ranks, hometowns, and missions. Anything to keep his brain occupied.

The most vital thing was communication. The prisoners invented a "tap" code. A certain number of taps on the wall stood for certain letters—the alphabet was divided up into fifths, without the letter "K," so one tap stood for the first row, and then another single tap for "A," two for "B," and so on. Their initial communications were begun with the old "Shave and a Haircut" cadence—tap, tap-ta tap-tap. Then the answer would come, "two bits," or tap-tap.

The other way the prisoners communicated was by holding a drinking cup to the wall and talking through it to the person on the other side. McCain "talked" in this way to a new prisoner who had been thrown in the cell next door. His name was Ernie Brace, and he was a civilian who had been shot down. He was probably working for the CIA, but that was never established, and McCain never asked him about it. Brace had been horribly treated by the North Vietnamese, and he was suspicious of everything, including the tap code and someone trying to talk to him through a drinking cup. But, eventually, McCain made contact with him, and they began to swap information.[21]

"As far as this business of solitary confinement goes—the most important thing for survival is communication with someone, even if it's only a wave or a wink, a tap on the wall, or to have a guy put his thumb up. It makes all the difference," McCain said in a first-person story he gave to *U.S. News and World Report* magazine shortly after his release from prison.[22]

THE OFFER

By mid-1968, life at the Plantation had settled into a macabre routine. The tap code was working, and prisoners kept track of one another. The guards were alternatively brutal and relatively benign. The prisoners learned that beatings were routine. When a few days passed without severe violence, they wondered what was up.

Interrogations—they were called "quizzes"—were also routine and generally elicited little information but lots of pain. McCain recalled one time when he was trussed up by ropes so that his arms were pulled behind his back, nearly out of their sockets, and he was left like that.

> One of the techniques they used from time to time was to take ropes and tie them around biceps and loop the rope around and put your arms between your legs. One night I was in that position and they had left me there for the night. The door to my cell opened and a guard walked in a gun guard, a sentry, who walked over to me put his finger to his lips and loosened the ropes that were binding me. About five hours later he came into the cell, at the end of his watch, tightened up the ropes and left, never saying a word.
>
> A few months later it was Christmas, Christmas Day. Because it was Christmas, they let us out, stand out of my cell for about 10 minutes. I went outside, standing there, who comes wandering over but the same guard . . . With his sandal he drew a cross on the dirt. He stood there looking at me, didn't say a word. After a few minutes, he rubbed it out with his sandal and walked away. My friends, I will never forget that man, I will never forget that moment, and I will never forget the fact that no matter where you are, no matter how difficult things are there is always going to be someone of your faith and your belief and your devotion to your fellow man who will pick you up and help you out and bring you through.[23]

Those incidents were few. Any time leniency was shown, the prisoners suspected that something was up. In June 1968, something was definitely up with McCain. Some of his captors summoned him to a meeting and asked if he wanted to go home. Shocked, McCain did not answer and finally said he would have to think it over.

"I was worried whether I could stay alive or not, because I was in rather bad condition. I had been hit with a severe case of dysentery, which kept on for about a year and a half. I was losing weight again," McCain said.

"But I knew that the [military] Code of Conduct says, 'You will not accept parole or amnesty,' and that 'you will not accept special favors.' For somebody to go home earlier is a special favor. There's no other way you can cut it."[24]

McCain did not know it at the time, but his father was about to be named Commander-in-Chief (Pacific), which would put him in overall charge of the Vietnam War. The appointment was somewhat controversial, because, while Vietnam was a war that involved all of the armed services, it was essentially a land war, and the senior McCain was an admiral in the Navy. Nonetheless, his superiors decided that McCain should have the command. Some who questioned the appointment may have worried that because his son was a prisoner, he might alter his decision making. They need not have worried. Later in the war, he would order bombings of Hanoi that struck just over his son's head. But he did visit the Demilitarized Zone between the North and South often, telling associates he felt closer to his son there.

Back in Hanoi, McCain had made his decision. The answer was no. He would not take early release. Flabbergasted, his North Vietnamese captors told him that President Johnson had ordered his release. McCain demanded papers; there were none. Then, they showed him a letter from Carol in which she said she wished he had been one of the prisoners released early. Still, the answer was no.

"With this 'The Cat,' who was sitting there with a pile of papers in front of him and a pen in his hand, broke the pen in two. Ink spurted all over. He stood up, kicked the chair over behind him, and said, 'They taught you too well. They taught you too well'—in perfect English, I might add," McCain said.

The guards threatened that it was now going to be very bad for McCain. They weren't exaggerating.

A couple of weeks later, the beatings began. The guards beat McCain everywhere on his body, rebreaking his arm, beating his bad knee, kicking him in the head and ribs. They left him tied up at night and in the morning began the process all over again. This went on for four days. McCain tried to commit suicide by tying a shirt around his neck and looping it through a window shutter. But the guards found him and stopped the attempt. Finally, McCain broke and agreed to write out a statement about how he had committed "black crimes" against the Vietnamese people.[25]

"Every man has his breaking point, I had reached mine," McCain said later. He could hardly live with the shame he perceived he had brought on his fellows, his country, and his service. None of them blamed him, but he was particularly hard on himself.

Years later, some political opponents of McCain would try to use the incident as an example of disloyalty on his part. No one who had not been part of that experience could have possibly understood. Orson Swindle, a fellow prisoner who was a political supporter of his as well, often came to McCain's defense.

"I am incredibly proud of him," Swindle said. "It is hard for most people to understand the closeness we have, the honor we have of just knowing each other. We were so isolated. It was maddening to wake up in a place where you can't do anything."[26]

THE HANOI HILTON

After his "confession," McCain was moved back to the "Hanoi Hilton," the Hoa Lo prison. He met Swindle there and would spend the rest of his confinement in that place. While no five-star hotel (McCain would often say it was a hotel where they didn't leave a mint on the pillow at night), the prison had a routine and some rules. Beatings were still common, food was still awful, but the prisoners could communicate with each other.

They narrated stories for each other, putting on "plays" of movies they recalled. McCain, perhaps the best read of the bunch, was great at it. He would recall movies he had seen and books he had read. One of the camp's favorites was *One-Eyed Jacks*, a 1961 movie in which Marlon Brando is beaten by a worthless sheriff, played by Slim Pickens. McCain and Swindle particularly liked the part where Brando calls Pickens a "scum-sucking pig."[27] It was, apparently, a metaphor for the kinds of things they would have liked to have called their captors.

At Christmas 1968, McCain gave the name calling a try. The North Vietnamese had set up a Christmas tableau for the prisoners, complete with a choir singing hymns. Photographers were brought in to record the bucolic scene. McCain decided to destroy the image, spraying the F-word around the room as the cameras rolled. Two days later, he was beaten again, the guards apparently deciding that they shouldn't administer the regular punishment on Christmas.

Richard Nixon, the Republican nominee, won the U.S. presidential election in 1968, promising to bring peace to Vietnam. He secretly began bombing nearby Cambodia but also began peace talks. The talks would go on for years, fruitlessly.

A year later, Christmas 1969, Carol and the children were spending the holiday with her family in Philadelphia. She decided to drop off some gifts at her friends, the Bookbinders, who had hosted her wedding to John. It was snowing, and the roads were bad. On the way home, she skidded off the road and crashed into a telephone pole. Both of her legs were crushed, her pelvis and arm broken. She had internal injuries. She drifted in and out of consciousness. She lived, but the next two years were full of medical treatments, including 23 operations. By the time it was over, she had lost four inches off her former height of five-foot-eight.

Some members of the Navy said she should try to get a message to John about the accident. No, she said, he's got enough to worry about.

Life at the prison was no picnic, but McCain and the rest of the prisoners tried to find ways to pass the time. There were only three women on the prison staff, a young woman the prisoners called "Queenie," a wizened old crone dubbed "Mammy Yokum," who ran the kitchen, and a kitchen worker dubbed "Shovel" for her flat profile. "Queenie" began to be the object of some fantasy for the prisons. McCain described her as a "pretty young girl" with long hair. The prisoners tried often to get a glimpse of her. One day, as McCain was peeking through the slats of a makeshift shower in the courtyard, trying to watch Queenie wash clothes as he was trying to wash himself with a cup and a tank of water, he slipped because of his injured leg and fell into the unlocked door and out into the courtyard, naked. As he scrambled to get back into the stall, a difficult maneuver because of his injuries, he gave the camp a good laugh. And that story was retold often, every time with humor, providing welcome amusement.[28]

Another year went by, and another. McCain staged his own Christmas service in 1971—his church background acquired at Episcopal High School was finally being put to good use.

By 1972, President Nixon had ordered a resumption of the bombing of North Vietnam. There had been a pause in the bombing for a while, and no one cheered the resumption more than the prisoners of war. Though their lives were in danger every time the bombs dropped, they were happy to hear the American armament striking the North Vietnamese.

"It was the most spectacular show I'll ever see," McCain said. "We had about a 120-degree view of the sky, and, of course, at night you can see all the flashes. The bombs were dropping so close that the building would shake. The SAMs [surface-to-air missiles] were flying all over and the sirens were whining—it was really a wild scene. When a B-52 would get hit—they're up at more than 30,000 feet—it would light up the whole sky.

"So we were very happy. We were cheering and hollering. The 'gooks' didn't like that at all, but we didn't give a damn about that."[29]

The bombings were particularly hard on Admiral McCain, however, because he knew his son was in Hanoi. He couldn't stop the bombs; all he could do was pray.

"Every night he would pray on his knees," Roberta said. "I have a prayer book, an Episcopal prayer book, and you know that over time your hands would finally wear the papers out. Those pages were eventually worn out."[30]

NEGOTIATIONS AND RELEASE

Finally, in January 1973, the delegates to the peace talks between the United States and North Vietnam negotiated a cease-fire agreement. Henry Kissinger, Nixon's Secretary of State and foreign policy adviser, was the negotiator for the United States.

Things began to change a bit for the prisoners, as well. They sensed something was up, despite their lack of information. On January 20, 1973, McCain was moved from the Hanoi Hilton back to the Plantation.

Later, he learned that, while Kissinger had been signing the peace accords, he had been offered the chance to take McCain back to the United States with him. He refused. McCain was grateful.

"He, of course, refused, and I thanked him very much for that, because I did not want to go out of order. Most guys were betting that I'd be the last guy out—but you never can fathom the 'gooks,'" McCain said, using a derogatory term popular at the time.[31]

McCain was released on March 14 and was flown to the Philippines along with a group of other prisoners.

When she heard he was free, Carol called the children around to tell them that their daddy was coming home. In the years since John had been captive, Carol had filled the home with a menagerie of pets—dogs, cats, fish, gerbils, birds. Andy and Doug were elated. But Sidney, who was only six and had no memory of her father, was perplexed.

"Where will he sleep?" she asked, probably counting all of the living things in the house.

"He will sleep in my bed, with me," Carol said.

"And what will we feed him?" she asked.[32]

NOTES

1. John McCain with Mark Salter, *Faith of My Fathers* (New York: Random House, 1999), p. 189.

2. Ibid.

3. Paul Alexander, *Man of the People: The Life of John McCain* (New York: Wiley, 2003), pp. 47–49.

4. Associated Press, "McCain's Vietnam Rescuer Talks," February 4, 2000, http://quest.lubbockonline.com/stories/022400/gen_rescuer.shtml.

5. Robert Timberg, *John McCain: An American Odyssey* (New York: Free Press, 1999), p. 83.

6. Ibid., pp. 83–84.

7. McCain, *Faith of My Fathers*, p. 192.

8. Roberta McCain, interview with author, Washington, DC, April 15, 2008.

9. Ibid.

10. Joseph McCain, interview with author, Washington, DC, April 11, 2008.

11. R. W. Apple Jr., "Adm. McCain's Son, *Forrestal* Survivor, Is missing in Raid," *New York Times*, October 28, 1967, p. 1; "Pentagon Confirms Capture," *New York Times*, October28, 1967 (late edition), p. 4.

12. Joseph McCain, interview with author, Washington, DC, April 11, 2008.

13. Roberta McCain, interview with author, Washington, DC, April 15, 2008.

14. Dan Nowicki and Bill Muller, "McCain Profile: Chapter 3: Prisoner of War," *Arizona Republic*, March 1, 2007, http://www.azcentral.com/news/specials/mccain/articles/0301mccainbio-chapter3.html.

15. Roberta McCain, interview with author, Washington, DC, April 15, 2008.

16. McCain, *Faith of My Fathers*, p. 200.

17. McCain, *Hard Call: The Art of Great Decisions* (New York: Hachette, 2007), pp. ix–xiii.

18. Ibid., pp. xii.

19. George "Bud" Day, McCain campaign video, www.johnmccain.com.

20. McCain, *Faith of My Fathers*, p. 204.

21. Ernest C. Brace, "Messages from John," *The Wall Street Journal*, May 2, 2008.

22. John McCain, "John McCain, Prisoner of War: A First-Person Account," *U.S. News & World Report*, May 1973, http://www.usnews.com/articles/news/2008/01/28/john-mccain-prisoner-of-war-a-first-person-account_print.htm.

23. John McCain for President 2008, "Courageous Service," video advertisement, created August 30, 2007.

24. McCain, "John McCain, Prisoner of War: A First-Person Account."

25. Alexander, *Man of the People*, p. 60.

26. Orson Swindle, interview with author, September 1999, aboard the McCain campaign bus, New Hampshire.

27. Nowicki and Muller, "McCain Profile: Chapter 3: Prisoner of War."

28. McCain, *Faith of My Fathers*, p. 296.

29. McCain, "John McCain, Prisoner of War: A First-Person Account."

30. Roberta McCain interview, *CBS Evening News with Katie Couric*, May 9, 2008.

31. McCain, "John McCain, Prisoner of War: A First-Person Account."

32. Timberg, *John McCain: An American Odyssey*, p. 114.

Chapter 6

COMING HOME

Sidney's innocent question unwittingly summed up the strange situation John McCain found himself in as he limped down the airplane stairs to the runway at Clark Air Force Base in the Philippines. Deciding what to "feed" McCain would be only the first question to be asked.

He was entering a world that had gone on for five and one-half years mostly outside his knowledge. The prisoners had been given "bad" news from the United States—reports of war protests, the assassinations of Democratic presidential candidate Robert F. Kennedy and civil rights legend Martin Luther King in 1968, for example—but knew nothing of the "good" news. They had heard about American astronauts landing on the moon in 1969 only in the context of a war protestor saying that if America could land a man on the moon, why couldn't it end the Vietnam War?

Doctors attended to McCain's most obvious needs first, fitting him with a false tooth to replace the one that had been knocked out and getting him ready to be reunited with his family. Since he hadn't been told about Carol's accident, that was to be the first order of business, but an enlisted man let it slip first. He called home, and Carol told him she had been badly disfigured. "Well, you know, I don't look so good myself," McCain said.[1]

But he was already something of a celebrity. The *New York Times* trumpeted his return with a picture and included him in their story about the return of 108 prisoners of war, calling him one of the "more notable" prisoners to be released and mentioning his father, who had been commander. McCain was met at the plane by Admiral Noel Gaylor, his father's successor as commander in chief, Pacific (CINCPAC).[2]

Admiral McCain had suffered a mild heart attack in 1972. He had continued as CINCPAC after that but was relieved in 1973 by Gaylor. Pictures of McCain walking across the tarmac show him accompanied by Gaylor, with the broadest of smiles on the admiral's face.

McCain went to Jacksonville to be reunited with his family. It was something of a ragtag tableau, with three of the five family members on crutches: McCain, of course, with his still gimpy leg, leading the crew; Carol, still suffering from her massive accident; and 14-year-old Doug, who had broken a leg playing soccer. The headline on the *Jacksonville Times-Union* read: "No Limps in Joy of McCain Family Reunion."

That was the way it was supposed to be, the "and they lived happily ever after" storybook ending. But that wasn't reality. So many things had changed. McCain, himself, Carol, the kids who had grown so much without him—and his country, too, was different. POWs were generally treated better than many returning Vietnam veterans, who found that many in the country blamed them for the war—either for "losing" the war or for going there in the first place to fight a war that so many Americans didn't want. It was a confused and hurtful time in the nation, made more difficult by the Watergate scandal, which resulted in the resignation of President Nixon in 1974—the first time that had ever happened. Nixon lied about covering up a break-in at Democratic National Headquarters and a whole series of other "dirty tricks" and was about to be impeached and probably removed from office when he decided to quit, instead.

When McCain left for war, the music was rock 'n' roll—the Beach Boys, Jerry Lee Lewis, the early Beatles. By the time he came back, it was psychedelic, acid rock, Pink Floyd, and AC/DC. The country was sick of war, and the military had fallen out of favor.

McCain was 36 years old when he came home, much older than many of the Vietnam-era soldiers. He always maintained that when he left Vietnam, he left it all behind. Even he would admit that is a slight exaggeration, for he had changed immeasurably. For one thing, the carefree man/boy who had partied hard and kicked back often was gone. He retained the acerbic sense of humor and the devotion to country.

Once home, Carol and John began to slowly talk about the six years that had passed since they had seen each other. John recounted some of his tales of imprisonment. Carol filled him in on the kids and her own health. McCain asked Carol if there was anything she had not gotten while he was away. She wanted a beach house. He bought her a house on the ocean.[3]

Joe McCain remembers his brother and sister-in-law trying so hard to live together again. "They worked extremely hard to put it back together and couldn't," he said. "He expected to come back to this magical, beautiful, perfect place, and it wasn't there."[4]

It would turn out to be impossible, but they gave it a good try for a long time.

Meanwhile, McCain had to figure out the rest of his life and his career, as well. First, his physical injuries were such that Navy doctors and physical therapists told him he would never regain flight status because he couldn't bend his knee far enough. He needed to be able to bend it 90 degrees. He had about 10 degrees at most in the beginning. A private physical therapist, Diane Rauch, heard about the crippled POW and, out of the blue, offered to help. McCain couldn't pay her. She did it for free. The painful treatment went on for months, but McCain finally got his 90 degrees. And Diane? Well, she married McCain's friend and fellow POW Bill Lawrence.

With the therapy, he was cleared to fly again. It was probably a generous clearance, because, in addition to the knee problems, he couldn't raise his arms above his shoulders because of all the torture. He probably couldn't have even reached up to pull the ejection seat handle if it had ever come to that again.

He still wanted to stay in the Navy but was already beginning to think about a career outside the military: "If I have to leave the Navy, I hope to serve the Government in some capacity, preferably in Foreign Service for the State Department. I had a lot of time to think over there [in Vietnam] and came to the conclusion that one of the most important things in life—along with a man's family—is to make some contribution to his country."[5]

With the physical part of his rehabilitation done, he turned to the intellectual part. He decided he would go to the Navy War College and study the war in Vietnam. He had become intensely curious about the war that had so radically changed his life. Why did the United States get into the war in the first place? Why was it fought the way it was? Why did it eventually end in defeat for the United States?

Because the military was showing plenty of deference toward POWs, McCain expected to have no difficulty going to the war college. What he hadn't counted on was that his rank, lieutenant commander, wasn't high enough. He had been selected for commander, the next highest rank and the one that would qualify him for the war college, but the promotion was taking a while to come through. He was told he couldn't go. However, McCain was determined, and he decided to pull strings. He contacted the secretary of the navy, John Warner, who was a friend of his father's, and pleaded his case. He got the war college appointment. Years later, McCain would serve in the Senate alongside Warner, who became a senator from Virginia.

McCain studied for nine months at the war college and wrote a thesis about the Code of Conduct for prisoners that would reflect the Vietnam War experience. He concluded that the war was not wrong, just wrongly fought. "I was not an embittered veteran before I entered the War College, nor am I now. But I did resent how badly civilian leaders had mismanaged the war and how ineffectually our senior military commanders had resisted their mistakes. More appalling to me was how Americans had let the least fortunate among us fight the war for them, while sons of privilege were afforded numerous opportunities to stay home. That was a political decision made not just by the president, Congress and the services, but by the country as a whole and I resented the hell out of it."[6]

And he also learned a broader theme about war and the American people, a theme that would stay with him through other positions and wars to come.

"I learned a very important lesson that you cannot pursue a conflict that the American people will not support over time," McCain said. "They will be patient, but over time they will not support foreign military operations that risk American lives unless you show them a path of success."[7]

In his thesis, he expressed the desire that the American government do a better job of explaining "foreign policy." It appears that he was trying to figure out a way to prevent the country from opposing a war as vigorously as it had the Vietnam War. He also suggested that the code be modified to say that prisoners should "make every reasonable effort" to escape, rather than "every effort." He was taking his experience to heart and using it to make the code a bit more practical. He also suggested that if prisoners were forced to make statements, the U.S. government should assume that all of those statements had been made under torture or otherwise coerced.[8]

McCain's next step was to find a "real" job in the Navy. Having gotten his promotion, he was fit for a command, and near the end of 1974 he was made commanding officer of VA 174, a replacement air group that trained carrier pilots at Cecil Field in Jacksonville, Florida. It was a post that was usually given to officers with more experience than McCain, and it was no secret that some skeptical Navy officers wanted him to fail. Unfortunately for them, McCain was a spectacular success.

He promised that if he was given authority to take parts from one aircraft and put them into another, he would be able to get the entire air wing flying. Skeptical superiors gave him the go-ahead to try. He did it. By the time he finished his tour there, every plane was flying. He credited his fliers, test pilots, and maintenance crews with getting the squadron fully operational. They credited him.

The VA 174 received its first ever Meritorious Unit Citation. There was more to the success of McCain's effort than just the success of the squadron. At a time when military service was at its lowest point in memory, the achievement gave the Navy something to be proud of. "Of course, the squadron's purpose was to train aviators, but the men and women of VA 174 knew that they were serving a greater purpose: to demonstrate the resolve of the United States Navy to overcome the decline in morale and readiness that temporarily afflicted the military after the Vietnam War," McCain said years later.[9]

At the change of command that would relieve McCain of his duty to the squadron, McCain's father joined his mother, Carol, and the kids and listened as Admiral Kidd commemorated the change of command, comparing McCain favorably to his father and grandfather. "I have never cried easily, but I found it especially hard not to that day," McCain wrote.[10]

As much of a success as his military career had been, and despite the gathering of his family at the Jacksonville ceremony, McCain's marriage was tearing apart. He and Carol had become very different people from the ones they were when McCain went to Vietnam. And McCain had probably changed the most. By his own admission, he was carousing again, in a way that was not fitting for a married man. "My marriage's collapse was attributable to my own selfishness and immaturity more than it was to Vietnam, and I cannot escape blame by pointing a finger at the war. The blame was entirely mine," McCain said.[11]

It was very tough for a while for the couple. They separated but were not divorced when McCain met the woman who was to become his second wife, Cindy Hensley. The kids took even longer to adjust. But, somehow, McCain managed to eventually get on good terms with Carol.

"I'm crazy about John McCain and I love him to pieces," Carol McCain said in 2000 as McCain was making his first run for president, "but I'm just not going to do any interviews."[12]

After his successful tour in Jacksonville, McCain was assigned to a job that would point the direction of the rest of his career: the Navy's liaison to the U.S. Senate.

NOTES

1. Robert Timberg, *John McCain: An American Odyssey* (New York: Free Press, 1999), p. 115.

2. James P. Sterba, "POW Commander among 108 Freed," *New York Times*, March 15, 1973, p. 4.

3. Timberg, *John McCain: An American Odyssey*, p. 116.

4. Joseph McCain, interview with author, April 11, 2008, Washington, DC.

5. John McCain, "John McCain, Prisoner of War: A First-Person Account," *U.S. News & World Report*, May 1973, http://www.usnews.com/articles/news/2008/01/28/john-mccain-prisoner-of-war-a-first-person-account_print.htm.

6. John McCain with Mark Salter, *Worth the Fighting For* (New York: Random House, 2002), pp. 11–12.

7. John McCain, interview with author, Washington, DC, July 25, 2008.

8. John S. McCain, "Individual Research Project: The Code of Conduct and the Vietnam Prisoners of War," National War College, Washington, DC, April 8, 1974.

9. John McCain, campaign speech, "Service to America" tour, Cecil Field, Jacksonville, Florida, April 3, 2008, http://www.johnmccain.com/Informing/News/Speeches/f4e9442b-18fa-489c-8255-9d323db42542.htm.

10. McCain, *Worth the Fighting For*, p. 13.

11. Ibid., pp. 13–14.

12. Nicholas D. Kristof, "P.O.W. to Power Broker, A Chapter Most Telling," *New York Times*, February 27, 2000, http://query.nytimes.com/gst/fullpage.html?res=9B02EFDF1439F934A15751C0A9669C8B63&sec=&spon=&pagewanted=all.

Chapter 7

NAVY SENATE LIAISON

The title "Navy liaison to the Senate" doesn't exactly give much of an indication of what that job really is. Tucked away in a corner on the first floor of the Russell Senate Office Building, a nondescript office sits next to similar offices reserved for the other armed services. On paper, the Navy liaison officer is supposed to be the face of the Navy for the Senate. But, in reality, the job is part lobbyist (though technically the military services aren't supposed to lobby), part tour director, part public relations man. The Navy thought it would be a good job for McCain because he already had a high profile as a former POW. McCain had a role model for the job because his father had once held it. But McCain made the job into much, much more.

For the four years that he held the job, 1977–1981, his office became a fun place to go for members of the Senate. McCain was always ready with a bit of food or drink and, better yet, witty and stimulating conversation. The man who wouldn't shut up after two years in solitary confinement was continuing to be a fabulous conversationalist.

"To have gone through the experiences he did, and to be tortured, some people might have been more solitary, more inward-looking, more dark," said William Cohen, who was a senator from Maine during the time McCain served as Navy liaison and who became one of his best friends. "John was the opposite. He told great stories and jokes on himself. You want to be in the presence of people who are so positive, and who have such a 'joie de vivre' [love of life]."[1]

Besides which, McCain was interested in everything. He soaked up information as he had when he was cramming for exams back at the Naval

Academy, but now he was in a much different position. He was the Navy's eyes and ears on Capitol Hill. And he intended to make the most of it.

Along the way he stroked a political itch. In the back of his mind there was always the possibility of going into politics, but McCain really had never seen how politics worked up close. Now, he was in the thick of it, and, from all accounts, he was comfortable with what he saw. It was as if he saw the senators, up close, with all of their strengths and weaknesses and began to think that he could do that too, as least as well as they could.

What he saw influenced him "a lot. I saw senators who worked hard and really knew what they were doing affected Americans. I saw young senators who really knew the issues who would go to the floor of the Senate and . . . propose legislation that had a profound impact—both positive and negative. It motivated me to find out whether I could embark on that path."[2]

It was his real entry into the world of politics.

He had dipped a toe into the political world a bit before, giving speeches at various events, invited by groups who wanted to hear his POW story. And he had met Ronald and Nancy Reagan in 1973, when Reagan was governor of California. Reagan had taken an interest in the returning POWs and, through a set of intermediaries, arranged to meet John and Carol.

Reagan wanted to hear about prison. McCain told him stories—glossing over some of the more difficult parts. Reagan invited McCain to speak at a prayer breakfast in Sacramento in 1974, Reagan's last year as governor. "Nancy cries when we send out the laundry," Reagan said, in introducing McCain. "So I want to tell you, she'll never make it through listening to a talk by our next guest, Commander John McCain."

McCain told about despair in prison and of seeing a scratching on the prison wall: "I believe in God, the Father Almighty."

Nancy Reagan, and not a few others, had the tissues out before McCain could finish the story.[3]

In the Senate, senators found they liked being around McCain. They began to ask that he accompany them on foreign trips, which was part of the job, but McCain was much more than a bag carrier. He was viewed almost as an equal by many senators, especially those who were close to him in age, particularly Cohen, the Maine Republican who would go on to be Secretary of Defense, and Gary Hart, a Colorado Democrat who would run, unsuccessfully, for president.

Hart remembered McCain as a "fascinating character" who was "fun to be around." His office "was the place that you could go and put your feet up."[4]

Hart, Cohen, and McCain cemented their friendship on a trip to Asia in 1978. It was the first official Senate delegation to visit China in the wake of a thaw in relations between China and the United States. They went to many briefings—Cohen remembers being assigned the difficult topic of human rights to discuss with Chinese Communist dictator Deng Tsao Ping—but they also found time for fun.

They found time to take in Tokyo's "Ginza" nightclub district and to visit the Temple of the Reclining Buddha in Bangkok.[5]

"It was three young guys enjoying the trip," Cohen said.[6]

In Washington, John and Carol McCain often entertained in their home, the lively dinner parties masking marital troubles that almost no one knew about.

Along with Hart and Cohen, McCain made two friends in the U.S. Senate who perhaps had even more influence on him—particularly underscoring the idea that politicians can make a difference.

The first was Senator Henry "Scoop" Jackson, a Democrat from Washington State. Jackson was a Cold War Democrat and a strong advocate for national defense. He supported the war in Vietnam, even after its end, and was always curious to hear about McCain's experiences. He was also a strong supporter of Israel. A quiet and unassuming man, he was described by many as "boring." But he was also intelligent and curious. In the early 1970s, an informal poll of his Senate colleagues ranked him best qualified to be president, yet Jackson was unsuccessful in his 1972 and 1976 bids for the Democratic Party's presidential nomination. He was a much better senator than he was a candidate.[7]

McCain admired Jackson greatly, especially for his work on arms control treaties, which McCain mistrusted, and in foreign policy, especially in opening up relations with China and working for human rights. Jackson was an ardent anti-Communist who believed that Communist countries like the Soviet Union would eventually fail. Years later, he was proven right. From Jackson, McCain learned that senators could make a huge difference in the state of the world.

The other senator who McCain came to admire was John Tower, a Texas Republican, Tower and Jackson led the Senate Armed Services Committee, so it was natural that McCain would gravitate to Tower, as well. But the two became more than close professionals; they were friends, and some said it was something of a father/son relationship. They enjoyed each other's company and would often be found late at night sharing a drink in Tower's office, which was right around the corner from McCain's.

They traveled together often. As part of his role as trip organizer, McCain always made sure that Tower had liquor in his room—even in countries where strong drink was prohibited. Years later, Tower's drinking and alleged womanizing would get him into major trouble when he was nominated for Secretary of Defense (the nomination was rejected), but in those days McCain and he would drink often.

On a trip to Oman in 1979 with Tower, McCain committed a social faux pas by sitting on the ground with his feet sticking out in front of him, the soles of his feet clearly visible. Everyone else was sitting cross-legged, but, because of McCain's injuries, he couldn't cross his legs. Exposing the soles of one's feet to the sultan was considered an extreme insult by the Omanis. Tower came to McCain's rescue, explaining to the Sultan that McCain had been gravely injured in the war. The sultan, a military man himself, understood. McCain was grateful, but Tower never let him forget about the time he "saved my life in the Omani desert." They kidded about it for years.[8]

From Tower, McCain learned about the ability to influence foreign and military policy from the Senate. The shapes of his future political life were coming into focus.

By this time, Jimmy Carter, a Democrat, had become president in 1976. Carter was determined to spend less money on the military since the United States was not at war. One of the things Carter did not want to do was build a new aircraft carrier. Many in the Senate wanted the new carrier, but others went along with Carter. McCain argued forcefully that the new carrier should be built, citing the fact that parts of the ship were built in many states all over the country, providing good jobs in many places, not just at the Newport News, Virginia, Shipyard—and some give him credit for saving the carrier. Carter vetoed one bill that included money for the carrier but eventually signed another one that included funds for it. While McCain downplayed his role, he played a behind-the-scenes part.[9]

While his power behind the scenes in the Senate was increasing, the power to keep his marriage together was fading. He and Carol continued to maintain a façade of a home, but he was spending more and more time away. Part of that was because of the nature of his job, but part of it was that the two were growing further apart.

They separated (though not legally) in 1979, when McCain was nearly 40 years old. Carol would say later that while John was 40, he wanted to be 25 again.

McCain was in Honolulu in late 1979 on a stopover with a Senate delegation he was escorting to China. At a reception, he met Cindy Lou Hensley, the only child of a wealthy Arizona beer distributor. He was 42; she was 24. They both lied about their ages. He subtracted four years from his; she added four years to hers. The two would joke about that for years. "We found out when we applied for a marriage license," Cindy Mc-Cain said. "They publish that in the newspaper in Arizona. That's how we found out how old we were. It doesn't matter. We started our marriage on a tissue of lies," she joked to Jay Leno on the *Tonight* TV show.[10] McCain has told the same story over and over.

Cindy Hensley was beautiful, blond, and young, but she was no vacant beauty queen. She was teaching learning-disabled children when John McCain met her, a job she did not need but apparently loved. She had graduated with honors from the University of Southern California and wanted to put her knowledge to use.

McCain deserted his delegation to spend the rest of the evening with Cindy. He talked about her for the rest of the trip and, when he got back, began making time to see her over the next year. They got together in Washington, in Arizona, and in other places.

While some have questioned McCain's motives in taking up with a young, rich, beautiful woman, McCain says simply, "I was in love." He also notes that Cindy's parents were very accepting of him and gracious about the match.[11] Even Carol, his former wife, does not question his motives in taking up with Cindy, except to say that he was trying to be younger and Cindy was young.

"It was a new life," Bill Cohen said. "I saw him after he met Cindy Lou, as we called her then, and he told me he was in love with her."[12]

Carol and John McCain were legally separated in January 1980 and divorced in February. In May, Cindy Hensley and John McCain were married in Phoenix. Bill Cohen was his best man, and Gary Hart was in the wedding party. The two honeymooned in Hawaii, where they first met.

Carol, meanwhile, had gone to work for Nancy Reagan as a campaign assistant while Ronald Regan was running for president. The press corps traveling with the Reagans knew all about Carol's marital breakup and attempted to cheer her up. When Ronald Reagan made a speech at the Alamo, in Texas, asking where all the heroes of yesteryear had gone, Lou Cannon of the *Washington Post* slipped up behind her and quipped, "Yeah, where is that SOB?"[13]

But Carol was not bitter, and her children came around eventually. In the divorce settlement, McCain was generous, giving Carol the rights to houses in Florida and Virginia and agreeing to provide insurance or pay for any additional medical treatments Carol was expected to need.[14]

McCain was generous to the kids, too, and they all ended up campaigning for him in his first run for the presidency, in 2000. Andrew McCain went to work for Cindy's father's beer company later in his life, rising to the position of chief financial officer. As with many other aspects of his life, notably Vietnam, McCain didn't look backward; he moved ahead.

McCain was facing another crossroads in his life, as well—what to do about his Navy career. His physical injuries were making it more and more difficult for him to retain flight status. The odds of his making admiral like his father and grandfather were becoming longer, and he was not sure that was what he wanted, anyway.

In late 1980, McCain informed the Chief of Naval Operations that he was planning to retire. That was the easy part. The hard part was telling his father, by now retired himself and in increasingly poor health. Admiral McCain did not criticize his son's decision, though he told him to think it over. But McCain knew his father was disappointed. "When I left him that day, alone in his study, I took with me his hope that I might someday become the first son and grandson of four-star admirals to achieve the same distinction," McCain wrote later. McCain knew he would not achieve that status, even if he stayed in the Navy, but, since his father's ambition was to be admiral, "he must have grieved to know that it was not mine."[15]

Jack McCain died March 22, 1981, while on an airplane returning from a trip to Europe with Roberta. While he had been in ill health since he retired from the Navy in 1972, suffering from a series of seizures, he still liked to travel. Navy officials tried to reach McCain to tell him of his father's death but couldn't, so they called Carol. She was the one to tell John that his father had died, "which she did with great kindness and tact," McCain wrote.[16]

The funeral was a blur for McCain but was carried off with great military pomp. Admiral John S. McCain Jr. was buried at Arlington National Cemetery, near where his own father lay.

As if it were not enough to bury his father that day, McCain was making another momentous change as well—he was resigning from the Navy. He wore his uniform to the funeral service but never again. He turned in the trappings of Navy service and flew with Cindy to Arizona, where he was to be hired as a public relations man in her dad's company. And it was there that he began thinking about politics in earnest.

NOTES

1. William S. Cohen, interview with author, Washington, DC, July 9, 2008.

2. John McCain, interview with author, Washington, DC, July 25, 2008.

3. Robert Timberg, *John McCain: An American Odyssey* (New York: Free Press, 1999), p. 125.

4. Linda Douglass, "McCain's Turning Point," *National Journal*, April 26, 2008, pp. 24–28.

5. Dan Nowicki and Bill Muller "McCain Profile: Chapter 4: Back in the USA," *Arizona Republic*, March 1, 2007, http://www.azcentral.com/news/specials/mccain/articles/0301mccainbio-chapter4.html.

6. William Cohen, interview with author, Washington, DC, July 9, 2008.

7. University of Washington libraries, Henry M. Jackson papers, http://www.lib.washington.edu/specialcoll/findaids/docs/papersrecords/JacksonHenry3560.html.

8. John McCain with Mark Salter, *Worth the Fighting For* (New York: Random House, 2002), pp. 30–31.

9. Douglass, "McCain's Turning Point."

10. *The Tonight Show with Jay Leno*, NBC, May 5 2008, http://youtube.com/watch?v=Hv7LUT1ezm0&feature=related.

11. McCain, *Worth the Fighting For*, p. 33.

12. William Cohen, interview with author, Washington, DC, July 9, 2008.

13. Timberg, *John McCain: An American Odyssey*, p. 140.

14. Dan Nowicki and Bill Muller "McCain Profile: Chapter 5: Arizona, the Early Years," *Arizona Republic*, March 1, 2007, http://www.azcentral.com/news/specials/mccain/articles/0301mccainbio-chapter5.html.

15. McCain, *Worth the Fighting For*, pp. 9–10.

16. Ibid., p. 5.

Chapter 8

RUNNING FOR CONGRESS

The place I lived the longest was Hanoi.

—*John McCain*

John McCain blew into Arizona with a beautiful new wife, a new job in his father-in-law's company, and unbridled ambition. He was looking for a place to run for Congress, and Arizona, with its growing population, looked like a good bet. The census of 1980 had determined that Arizona's population was increasing so much that it would get another congressional seat, and McCain was positioning himself to take advantage of this possibility when it occurred. But McCain had no idea where that new congressional district would be drawn in the state. He hoped it would be in the Phoenix area, but no one knew for sure.

Questions have been raised about whether McCain's marriage to Cindy was merely politically opportunistic. Did he court and marry the wealthy beer heiress just so he could have a platform from which to run for Congress? He has always denied it, and the facts of his life seem to indicate that his motives were not that crass. He always fell in love quickly (remember the Brazilian model), and his heart nearly always drove his head in these affairs. He was coming off the breakup of his marriage to Carol, and he was trying to live a new kind of life. Cindy was smart as well as beautiful and rich, and she fit into that new life nicely. Both his mother and her parents approved of the match, moreover, and that speaks well of it.

Even before he moved to Arizona, he began laying the groundwork. Senator Bill Cohen had introduced him to political consultant Jay Smith, who had done work for Cohen but also had ties to political candidates in Arizona, including Representative John Rhodes, the House minority leader at the time. Smith and McCain set up a lunch in which McCain explained his plan to move to Arizona and run for a seat in Congress that did not yet exist.

Smith, an experienced political hand, was somewhat taken aback.

"I thought the notion that someone would move to a state that they had no ties to and run for Congress the following year was perhaps overly ambitious and unrealistic," Smith remembered, chuckling at his bit of understatement. But Smith was very impressed with McCain nonetheless. McCain's sense of humor and articulateness got to Smith, just as they had gotten to Cohen, Hart, Tower, and many others involved in politics.[1]

Smith was intrigued. But it would be a while before he got to do his job for McCain.

Throughout 1981, McCain traveled around Arizona, shaking hands and introducing himself. He continued speech-making to local civic clubs but also made sure he was getting to know the political movers and shakers in the state—folks who might be in a position to help him should he find a way to run for the U.S. House.

His plans suffered a blow when the new congressional district was drawn in the Tucson area, in the southern part of the state, far from Phoenix, where he had located. It was one thing to move to his wife's hometown and try to run for Congress; it was another to pick up and move again to a part of the state where he had absolutely no ties. Disappointed, he stayed put and continued to work for the Hensley beer distribution company and to move around the state.

Then fate intervened again. House Minority Leader Rhodes, the Arizona Republican from Phoenix, who had served in the House for 30 years and as minority leader from 1973 to 1980, decided to retire. The later years of his career had not been easy for Rhodes. He became minority leader after President Richard Nixon selected then-Minority Leader Gerald Ford to be his vice president after the forced resignation of Vice President Spiro Agnew on corruption charges. Then, Rhodes was one of the Republicans who went to Nixon in 1974 to say that the president would lose any impeachment vote in the House and Senate and that he, too, should resign. The Republican Party was in disarray. Rhodes held on, hoping that Ronald Reagan, who was elected president in 1980, would sweep enough members of the GOP into the House to make him speaker. But the Republicans stayed in the minority, and Rhodes stepped down from his leadership post. He announced his retirement in January 1982.[2]

As Rhodes was announcing his retirement, McCain was on the phone to Smith while simultaneously listening to someone he had sent to the Rhodes press conference. As soon as it became clear Rhodes was getting out of Congress, McCain was jubilant. But there was another technical detail to be worked out. McCain didn't actually live in Rhodes's district—his home with Cindy was several miles away.

As Smith and McCain talked, another person came into the room. Smith heard McCain say to Cindy, "Did you get it?" Get what, wondered Smith. The answer was a house. The McCains had just bought a house in the first congressional district, represented by Rhodes.[3]

But that was just a procedural hurdle. The much more difficult task was actually running for the seat. He may have felt like he knew what elective office was like, by virtue of his close acquaintances in the Senate, but McCain had never run for anything. Some had suggested he should run for the state legislature first, but he couldn't meet the residency requirement for that, which required that he live in the state for a number of years. Besides, he was too impatient for that.

He wanted to announce his candidacy the same day that Rhodes made his resignation decision public, but he was persuaded to take some time to "explore" the possibility of running and to let curiosity build about him.

McCain formally announced his candidacy for the U.S. House on March 25, 1982. He was 45 years old, and, despite his lack of previous office, he touted himself as someone who knew how Washington worked by virtue of his four years as Navy Senate liaison. That experience was viewed as a plus for McCain, especially since he was trying to replace someone who had served a lifetime in Congress. He was described by the Arizona Republican as a "political newcomer" and a "former prisoner of war." He joined two other Republican candidates already in the race, State Senator Jim Mack and State Representative Donna Carlson West.[4] A fourth candidate, Ray Russell, a veterinarian and civic leader, would also run.

The *Arizona Daily Star*, another newspaper in the district, thought so little of McCain's candidacy that it placed the announcement story on page E4, next to the comics. McCain liked to joke that he had three percent name recognition—that is, three percent of the voters knew who he was—in a poll with a three percent margin of error

The district was overwhelmingly Republican, so whoever won the Republican primary was a shoo-in for the seat.

McCain was undeterred by the fact that few people knew him and that fewer took him seriously. He just decided to outwork them. Smith gave him lists of Republican voters in the district, and he walked, door-to-door, six hours a day, six days a week, meeting voters. He would follow up the visits with a personal letter to everyone he met and then another letter on Election Day. He knocked on 20,000 Republican doors, trudging through neighborhoods in typical Phoenix 115-degree summer heat. He wore through two pairs of shoes.

But there was another weapon deployed in the race—television advertising. Because of McCain's connections to other senators and because he was plugged into the Phoenix business community, he was able to raise enough money to buy television time. That was relatively rare in House races at the time.

McCain raised $313,000 for the primary—more than half of it from loans to himself. That doesn't sound like a lot of money, but it was in 1982. The money bought TV ads. Smith recalled that the ads touted McCain's Washington experience, called him a "new leader for Arizona," and told the story of his POW days. "The ads gave him much wider exposure," Smith said. "To get known, you had to get on television. It was a critical advantage he held in that race."[5]

McCain made many joint appearances with the other three candidates in the Republican primary, and they all stood together for questions from the audience. One issue dogged McCain constantly—the carpetbagger issue. He was not from Arizona, and he had barely lived there a year. How could he even pretend to represent them? Time after time, he answered the question, recounting that he had retired from the Navy and moved to his wife's home state. One night, he lost his patience.

"Listen, pal," he snapped to the questioner. "I spent twenty-two years in the Navy. My father was in the Navy. My grandfather was in the Navy. We in the military service tend to move a lot. We have to live in all parts of the country, all parts of the world. I wish I could have had the luxury, like you, of growing up and living and spending my entire life in a nice place like the First District of Arizona, but I was doing other things.

"As a matter of fact, when I think about it now, the place I lived the longest in my life was Hanoi."

Wham. There it was. That was the answer. The crowd was stunned. And the race was over.

Smith's shrewd assessment was that McCain killed two election birds at once—he deflected the carpetbagger issue, and he cemented his image as a former prisoner of war. McCain says the response was completely spontaneous, that he'd heard that question about 10 times too many, and that he finally just came out with the answer.[6]

McCain wasn't done. One of his opponents, Jim Mack, had attempted to contact Carol McCain in an effort to dig up dirt on McCain. But Carol wouldn't play along. She told Mack that she wished McCain good luck.

When McCain found out that Mack had approached his ex-wife, he was furious. He confronted the candidate at one of the joint meetings and told him that if he ever caught wind of something similar happening ever again, he would personally beat the crap out of him.[7]

They still had to run the election, of course, and McCain was a wreck on Election Day. He decided to go to the movies (to see *Star Wars*) to get his mind off the election—the one day in a campaign when there's little for the candidate to do. He went to the movies every election after that, just for good luck.

When the votes were counted, McCain won the four-way contest with 32 percent of the vote; Russell got 26 percent; Jim Mack got 22 percent; and Donna Carlson West got 20 percent of the vote.[8]

The next morning, he was out campaigning again, fulfilling a campaign promise rashly made since it turned out he'd gotten no sleep the night before. But he doggedly hit the campaign trail and also secured endorsements from the three candidates he beat.

In the general election, McCain whipped Democrat William Hegarty, 66 percent to 31 percent. He was going back to Washington.

NOTES

1. Jay Smith, interview with author, Arlington, Virginia, July 7, 2008.

2. Bart Barnes, "John J. Rhodes Dies: Led GOP in House During Watergate," *Washington Post*, August 26, 2003, p. B4.

3. Jay Smith, interview with author, Arlington, Virginia, July 7, 2008. Also, Robert Timberg, *John McCain: An American Odyssey* (New York: Free Press, 1999), p. 144.

4. Don Harris, "Former Prisoner of War Declares Candidacy for 1st District," *Arizona Republic*, March 5, 1982, p. B1.

5. Jay Smith, interview with author, Arlington, Virginia.

6. John McCain, interview with author, Washington, DC, July 25, 2008.

7. Timberg, *John McCain: An American Odyssey*, p. 149.

8. Alan Ehrenhalt, *Politics in America 1984* (Washington, DC: CQ Press, 1983), pp. 55–56.

Chapter 9

CONGRESSMAN

McCain arrived back in Washington determined to be seen as the congressman from Arizona. He *was* the congressman from Arizona, of course, but many of his constituents were still skeptical of this newly minted Arizonan and figured that once he got back to Washington he would forget all about them. He had a steep learning curve to familiarize himself with Arizona issues, and he was still balancing his Washington experience against his Arizona responsibilities.

The first thing that happened to him was that he got elected president of the freshman class of House members. That title, which reflects little more than a beauty contest, usually goes to someone with some experience or notoriety, and he had that. He also was proving that his gregariousness on the campaign trail and as a Navy liaison in the Senate would translate well to the House of Representatives.

His first speech on the House floor, in January 1983, showed how comfortable he was to be in Congress. He read an excerpt from Tom Wolfe's *The Right Stuff*, the definitive book on the early astronauts in the U.S. space program, about the feeling a young man had finding "himself all at once enclosed in a fraternity" when he joined the space program.[1]

If he was beginning to feel too comfortable, however, his old POW buddy Orson Swindle was there to bring him straight down to Earth. Swindle and McCain were both fans of the old cartoon show *Felix the Cat*, which ran on American television in the 1960s. When Felix would get into trouble, he would put his paws to his face and rock back and forth with a sheepish grin. Imitating that grin kept Swindle and McCain laughing even in the darkest prisoner-of-war days. When McCain was sworn into office, it was Swindle's job to keep him humble. As McCain was moving into his first congressional office, at 1123 Longworth House Office Building, Swindle arrived with a gift—a stuffed Felix. Swindle told McCain, "When you get too big for your britches, always remember where you came from."[2]

McCain was placed on two committees that reflected his Arizona interests—Interior and Insular Affairs, which handles land management, mining, water resources, and Native American issues, and the Select Committee on Aging, which was important to Arizona's growing retiree population.

Victoria "Torie" Clarke, who joined McCain's office as press secretary in the summer of 1983, said that McCain gave her only one marching order, and it was to emphasize Arizona issues. "You make darn sure they know how hard I'm working," he admonished Clarke.[3]

McCain's first bills all related to his Arizona constituents, particularly Native Americans. He proposed to add a representative of Indian tribal government to the Commission on Intergovernmental Relations, and he wanted to modify the leases and contracts on the Maricopa Indian Reservation (that one was made into law), and to modify the tax status of Indian tribal governments.

McCain insisted on putting his chief of staff in Tempe, Arizona, and on flying back to Arizona every weekend. He left Washington on Thursday night and returned, taking the overnight red-eye Tuesday morning. It was a grueling pace, but he insisted that would help cement his Arizona ties. Cindy remained in Arizona, as well.

"How can we be present in Washington around the clock and at the same time fulfill our commitment to remain close to our districts?" McCain wrote in a brief essay, "The Job of a Congressman Requires Redefining."[4]

McCain concentrated on other issues important to Arizonans. One of them was a bill to ban helicopter flights over the Grand Canyon, an issue important to environmentalists. He brought people into his office constantly to teach him about Arizona issues. There were maps spread on tables all over the office so that he could look at the expanse of the wild lands in comparison to the populated areas and get an idea of their impact.[5]

His trips back to Arizona allowed him to keep collecting allies, as well as tending to important issues. One ally was land developer Charles Keating, who became a major donor and a professional friend. That association would one day come back to haunt McCain, but at the time Keating was a valuable associate as well as one of the biggest employers in the state through his company, American Continental Corp.

While most of his work in his early years in Congress was routine, McCain would vote against one bill that would cause him problems later as he expanded his range on political issues. In August 1983, McCain voted against a bill to establish a federal Martin Luther King Day holiday. He was in the distinct minority on the issue, as the bill, which had been debated for 15 years and rejected previously, passed the House 338–90. Republicans were almost evenly split, however, 89–77.[6] Most of McCain's Arizona colleagues also voted against the bill, giving him some political cover, because the issue was controversial in his state. But McCain would say in later years that he was wrong to cast a "no" vote, and he gave his full support to establishing a state King holiday in Arizona.

Also, while in Washington, McCain tended to military issues, introducing a bill to provide for the expansion and improvement of the national cemeteries for veterans.

Pretty routine stuff for a rookie, but getting on the Interior Committee would prove to be far more important that it would seem initially for the simple reason that it brought McCain in contact with the man who would take him under his wing and turn him into a much more knowledgeable representative of Arizona. That man was Morris "Mo" Udall.

MO

Mo Udall was a self described "one-eyed Mormon Democrat from conservative Arizona."[7] He was chairman of the Interior Committee in the House and a member of a prominent Arizona family that traced its roots back to pioneers in covered wagons. He lost his eye in a childhood accident, but it never slowed him down. He had run for president once, disastrously, but was a leader in the House. He was a gentle man, not a fierce partisan, and a tireless crusader for Arizona issues. He had won the respect of almost every member of the House, whether they agreed with him or not.

The traditions of "to get along, go along" were dying in the House. A new brand of fiery conservative Republicans, led by Representative Newt Gingrich of Georgia, was coming into ascendancy in the House, muscling aside traditional leader like House Minority Leader Bob Michel of Illinois and even senior Democrats like Udall. McCain was invited to join Gingrich's "Conservative Opportunity Society," which would have fit his politics since he was largely a "Ronald Reagan Conservative," but he declined. Udall, far senior to McCain and in charge of an important agenda, also could have ignored McCain, but he didn't.

Udall decided he wanted to emphasize Indian affairs, and he wanted McCain to work with him. They made up an ad hoc committee—an informal panel—to deal with this issue. During McCain's first year in Congress, the two held a press conference in Casa Grande, Arizona. Udall prefaced many of his remarks with "Congressman McCain and I." McCain, by his own admission, had little to do with the issues Udall was addressing. It was generous for Udall to give him partial credit. "I barely understood the difference between the U.S. Forest Service and the Bureau of Land Management and couldn't tell a copper mine from a cotton farm," McCain wrote.[8]

McCain sponsored two bills with Udall—one in 1984 that added 1 million acres to the wilderness area established by Udall legislation in 1964 and another that set aside 1.4 million acres of Arizona desert wilderness. The latter bill came after McCain had gone to the Senate.

One of the things that brought the two together—other than shared interest—was their sense of humor. Udall's was dry, acerbic, and very funny. He referred to himself as "ole second-place Mo" after finishing runner-up in many presidential primaries in 1976. "Not everyone can come in first," he once said. "Even George Washington married a widow."[9] He also gave McCain one of his best campaign lines that he would use much later. Noting that both he and Arizona Senator Barry Goldwater (in 1964) had run unsuccessfully for president, Udall quipped, "Arizona is the only state in the union where mothers don't tell their children that anyone can grow up to be president."

After McCain's unsuccessful run for president in 2000, he told the joke and added his name to the list. However, he modified it in his 2008 run for the highest office in the land, saying it might no longer apply.

Tragically, by 1980, Udall began suffering from Parkinson's disease and he died of complications from the illness in 1998. McCain visited Udall often, usually unannounced, and spent hours at his bedside, even when Udall's condition had deteriorated so much that he could no longer even acknowledge McCain's presence.[10]

LEBANON

McCain was mostly a reliable conservative supporter of President Ronald Reagan, stemming both from his ideas and from his personal relationship with the president. But he was beginning to show an independent "maverick" streak even then, born of his life experience. He supported Reagan's issues 80 percent of the time in 1983, but that support was down to 64 percent of the time by 1985.[11]

McCain supported Reagan's tax cuts, and he went along with the president's hard stand against Communism in the Soviet Union. But on one important issue, he broke ranks. Reagan had sent American Marines into Lebanon, which had been wracked by civil war, to serve as peacekeepers. Despite the multinational force, there continued to be no peace in Lebanon. By the fall of 1983, the battleship USS *New Jersey* had been stationed off the coast of Beirut, Lebanon, and the American involvement continued to escalate. Despite it all, the civil war raged on.

The Reagan administration had contended that the Marine deployment fell short of a war effort and therefore didn't need the acquiescence of Congress. But pressure was building, and Congress finally began to debate a resolution to formally authorize the deployment. The Reagan administration had rounded up enough support to pass the resolution but, surprisingly to those who thought he was a reliable supporter, not McCain's. He wrestled with the decision for weeks, contacting some of his most trusted advisers. He thought that the situation in Lebanon, a civil war, had overtones of the war in Vietnam, which was still deeply embedded in his consciousness. He didn't see a role for the United States, particularly not one for the force of 1,600 "peacekeepers" that he thought were too few to do any good, too many to be anything less than an inviting target for terrorists.

While Lebanon was not Vietnam, McCain could see no good in the United States being there. He decided to vote against the resolution, knowing that it would pass anyway but deciding not to go along. He informed House Minority Leader Michel and the White House, that he would not be with them this time.

On September 28, 1983, he rose on the House floor to make one of his rare speeches as a freshman member of Congress. Ears in the galleries and on the floor pricked up as it became clear what the new Republican was doing.

> Mr. Speaker, it is with great reluctance that I rise in opposition to this resolution. I am well known for my respect for the President of the United States and for supporting his policies. I do not believe the President should be restricted in fulfilling his constitutionally mandated responsibility of conducting our nation's foreign policy. However, when called on to make a judgment, as I am by this legislation, I have a responsibility to my constituents to carefully evaluate the alternatives, using whatever resources are at my command.
>
> I have agonized over this issue, not only because of my personal experiences but more importantly because of my training

in military doctrine, strategy, and tactics. . . . I have listened carefully to the explanations offered for our involvement in Lebanon. I do not find them convincing.

The fundamental question is: "What is the United States' interest in Lebanon?" It is said we are there to keep the peace. I ask, what peace? It is said we are there to aid the government. I ask, what government? It is said we are there to stabilize the region. I ask, how can the U.S. presence stabilize the region?

Since 1975 we have seen a de facto partition of Lebanon. I see little possibility of this changing any time soon. I ask you, will the Lebanese Army ever be strong enough to drive out the Syrians let alone the PLO [Palestine Liberation Organization]? If the answer to this question is no, as I believe it is, then we had better be prepared to accept a lengthy and deeper involvement in the area.

I ask my colleagues, what incentive is there for the Syrians to engage in constructive peace talks? What do they gain from a peaceful Lebanon? Do you really think naval forces off the Lebanese coast are going to intimidate the Syrians so much that they engage in meaningful negotiations? For this to occur the Syrians must believe we will use the full military power at our disposal. Are we prepared to use this power? I do not think so, nor do I believe the Syrians think so.

The longer we stay in Lebanon, the harder it will be for us to leave. We will be trapped by the case we make for having our troops there in the first place.

What can we expect if we withdraw from Lebanon? The same as will happen if we stay. I acknowledge that the level of fighting will increase if we leave. I regretfully acknowledge that many innocent civilians will be hurt. But I firmly believe this will happen in any event.

What about our allies and worldwide prestige? We should consult with our allies and withdraw with them in concert if possible, unilaterally if necessary. I also recognize that our prestige may suffer in the short term, but I am more concerned with our long-term national interests. I believe the circumstances of our original involvement have changed, and I know four American families who share this view.

I am not calling for an immediate withdrawal of our forces. What I desire is as rapid a withdrawal as possible.

> I do not foresee obtainable objectives in Lebanon. I believe the longer we stay, the more difficult it will be to leave and I am prepared to accept the consequences of our withdrawal. I will vote in opposition to this resolution.[12]

The resolution passed the House, 260–170. The Senate followed suit.

But McCain had re-ignited media interest in him. He was called on to debate Lebanon on programs like the *MacNeil/Lehrer NewsHour* on Public Television and articles about him appeared in the *New York Times* and the *Washington Post*.

On October 23, 1983, terrorists struck, almost as McCain had predicted. The Marines were the target. A Mercedes-Benz truck, loaded with a ton of dynamite, crashed into the front door of the Marine barracks in Beirut, where 400 Marines were sleeping. Two hundred forty-one Marines died. McCain took no pleasure in the events. He mourned with the rest of the nation, which would live with the consequences of those events for many years.

NOTES

1. Sasha Issenberg, "First Term Shaped McCain's Identity; Local Agenda Was Wellspring," *Boston Globe,* May 30, 2008, http://www.boston.com/news/nation/articles/2008/05/30/first_term_shaped_mccains_identity.

2. Paul Alexander, *Man of the People: The Life of John McCain* (Hoboken, NJ: Wiley, 2005), p. 97.

3. Torie Clarke, interview with author, Bethesda, MD, July 8, 2008.

4. Issenberg, "First Term Shaped McCain's Identity."

5. Torie Clarke, interview with author, Bethesda, MD, July 8, 2008.

6. Don Wolfensberger, "The Martin Luther King Holiday: The Long Struggle in Congress," Woodrow Wilson International Center for Scholars, January 14, 2008.

7. Richard Severo, "Morris K. Udall, Fiercely Liberal Congressman, Dies at 76," *New York Times,* December 14, 1998, http://query.nytimes.com/gst/fullpage.html?res=9E03E7DC173DF937A25751C1A96E958260&sec=&spon=&pagewanted=all.

8. John McCain with Mark Salter, *Worth the Fighting For* (New York: Random House, 2002), pp. 78–79.

9. Ibid., p. 70.

10. Ibid., p. 83.

11. Alan Ehrenhalt, *Politics in America 1986* (Washington, DC: Congressional Quarterly Books, 1985), pp. 55–56.

12. McCain, *Worth the Fighting For,* pp. 95–96.

Chapter 10

IN BARRY GOLDWATER'S FOOTSTEPS: SENATOR

All of those trips back and forth to Arizona paid off for McCain, and he was handily re-elected to the House in 1984 with 78 percent of the vote to Democrat Henry Braun's 22 percent. That year was also momentous personally for John and Cindy McCain, who welcomed their first child together, a girl they named Meghan. She would be joined, in 1986, by John Sidney IV (called Jack) and, in 1988, by a second son, James, known as Jimmy.

McCain was beginning to build a Washington reputation, and his notoriety was increased when he joined famed CBS newsman Walter Cronkite in February 1985 on a trip to Vietnam to commemorate the tenth anniversary of the end of the Vietnam War. Cronkite was an icon, the former anchor of the CBS *Evening News* in the 1960s and 1970s, when news came on once a day and only three major networks produced news programs. There was no 24-hour cable news and no Internet, so most Americans got their news from Cronkite or his counterparts at NBC and ABC.

When McCain went to Vietnam with Cronkite for the filming of the hour-long documentary "Honor, Duty and a Place Called Vietnam," his profile immediately increased. It was good publicity for someone who was rumored to be thinking of running for the Senate, when, as anticipated, veteran Senator Barry Goldwater of Arizona retired.

Cronkite and McCain went back to Truc Bach Lake, where McCain landed after ejecting from his airplane. There, they found a monument erected to celebrate McCain's being shot down. The inscription read "McCan [sic] . . . famous air pirate." With the cameras rolling, Cronkite introduced McCain to the gaggle of Vietnamese who had gathered to see the famous American journalist and his guest. McCain and Cronkite also went to the prison where McCain had been tortured. In the hour-long special program, McCain appeared calm and composed as he discussed what had happened to him, but it had to have been a wrenching emotional experience.

In the documentary, McCain is shown at the prison. "There was a great deal of pain here," he said. "There was a great deal of suffering, a great deal of loneliness. There was also a lot of courage displayed."[1]

At this point, McCain was also feeling that Vietnam needed to do more to answer questions about missing Americans from the war and that Vietnam had not been forthright about their fates. The missing Americans were an issue that would linger for many more years, and it, among other things, impeded the normalization of relations between the United States and Vietnam for a long time.

Back in the United States, McCain turned his attention to domestic issues, but nagging at him were the recurring rumors about Goldwater. Goldwater was one of a kind, a five-term U.S. senator who was first elected in 1953. He was the Republican Party's nominee for president in the 1964 election, and, though he lost in a landslide to Lyndon Johnson, he later emerged as a respected elder statesman who was credited with forming the modern Republican conservative movement.

He was also a believer in personal liberty, and he later disagreed with the neoconservatives who gained strength in the Republican Party after the presidency of Ronald Reagan and who pressed a conservative social agenda.

Goldwater announced his retirement in the spring of 1986. Most Arizonans, including McCain, believed that Arizona's Democratic governor, Bruce Babbitt, would run for the Senate, setting up a battle royal between Babbitt, who was very popular in the state, and McCain. But fortune smiled on McCain again, and Babbitt decided not to run for the Senate and instead focused on a future run for president.

McCain declared his candidacy for the Senate on March 19, 1985. By his own admission, the race was his to lose. He was becoming quite popular in the state, he had a national profile, he had had some legislative successes, and not only had Babbitt decided not to run, but a potential strong Republican opponent, Representative Bob Stump, also declined to make the race.

The Democrats chose Richard Kimball, an Arizona public utilities regulator, for their candidate. Kimball was an attractive candidate, well spoken and good looking, but he had a decidedly uphill battle in an overwhelmingly Republican state where he was not well known to begin with.

"Kimball had only three hopes for an upset: I might screw up monumentally on my own; an unforeseen scandal involving me could suddenly and publicly erupt; or he could try to clobber me in televised debates. None of those things happened, as events turned out. But, at times, I appeared to be doing my part to make it a close race," McCain wrote.[2]

McCain and Goldwater got along well enough, but McCain always had his doubts that Goldwater really liked him. Perhaps it was McCain's irreverence that got in the way. During one stop in the 1986 Senate campaign, he met up with Goldwater, who assured the former prisoner of war that if he, Goldwater, had been elected president in 1964 over Lyndon Johnson, McCain would not have spent time in a North Vietnamese prison camp. "I guess that's right," McCain replied. "It would have been a Chinese prison camp." Goldwater was not amused.[3]

But McCain's Senate election campaign appeared to be going swimmingly. He had the backing of Darrow "Duke" Tully, publisher of the *Arizona Republic* and the *Phoenix Gazette*. Tully had endeared himself to McCain by telling him stories of his own military service as an Air Force pilot in Korea and Vietnam. The two got along well, and McCain often wrote opinion columns in Tully's papers.

Thus, it was an incredible shock to the paper, to the citizens of Arizona, and, most especially, to McCain when Tully was unmasked as a fraud who had made up all of his war stories. He had never served in the military, much less as an ace pilot. Tully resigned. McCain was stunned, a little resentful and mostly regretful. Despite the outcome, McCain thanked Tully for his support and for his newspaper's editorial endorsement of him. And he still had an election campaign to run.[4]

While things were going quite well for McCain against Kimball, McCain was about to do one of the things he said he had to do to tempt failure—mess up on his own. During the summer of the campaign, he gave a speech to students at the University of Arizona in Tucson. He was exhorting the young people to vote, largely because, as a demographic group, they don't vote in as large numbers as other groups, such as senior citizens, a large number of whom tend to vote in every election.

As McCain recalls the story, he was urging the students to vote as reliably as their elders. That was fine as far as it went. But then he went a step too far. One of the better-known brands of retirement community, a company that had a large presence in Arizona because of the large number of retirees, was known as Leisure World. Trying to ingratiate himself with the college students, McCain described the retirement community as "Seizure World, where 97 percent of the people who live there come out to vote while the other three percent are in intensive care."[5]

The "Seizure World" comment haunted McCain. Kimball made the most of it by organizing a protest of senior citizens. In a close race, that kind of mistake could have made the difference. But the race was not close. Kimball had some quirks, too, like his penchant for sending out press releases with many typos and misspellings. And McCain had far more money than Kimball.

The race was beginning to gain national recognition, as well. Syndicated columnist George Will wrote that McCain "almost certainly" would win the seat.[6]

There was one last hurdle—a series of three debates. Kimball had been demanding that McCain debate him, and McCain, with a comfortable lead in the polls, had been resisting. But he could hold out no longer. Kimball knew that McCain had a temper, and he planned to try to bait him. He tried the "Seizure World," quip, but McCain parried it. He tried to say that McCain had been avoiding debates; it fell flat. But then Kimball hit on one comment that sent McCain's eyes flashing. Kimball noted that McCain, shorter than Kimball by about six inches, was standing on a riser. "You stand on a soapbox to make yourself appear to look taller," Kimball said. McCain held his tongue, but he privately got steamed when he saw his picture the next day with him standing on the riser.[7]

On election day, McCain continued his tradition of going to the movies. This time, he saw *Crocodile Dundee*. Nationally, the election was not a good one for Republicans, who lost seven incumbents and control of the Senate. But for McCain, it was a wonderful night. Kimball carried Apache, Greenlee, and Santa Cruz counties and came within 595 votes of McCain in Pima County (Tucson), the second most populous county in the state. But McCain carried everything else handily.[8]

He arrived in the Senate already comfortable with the place from his previous experience there. He seemed destined for more. Johnny Apple, who by now was the *New York Times's* leading political correspondent, wrote that McCain "now seems poised to emerge as a significant figure in national politics, as a member of the United States Senate."[9]

On January 3, 1987, McCain was sworn in as a U.S. Senator by Vice President George H. W. Bush. Though in the minority in the Senate, he was already being talked about as a potential vice presidential candidate in 1988, with Bush at the top of the ticket. Big things were expected of him. He would get a seat on the Armed Services Committee, where he once had sat behind the dais, advising senators on how to question military witnesses. Now, he would get to do it himself.

He kept up his interest in Native American issues with a seat on the Select Committee on Indian Affairs. And he took a seat on the Senate

Commerce, Science and Transportation Committee to round out his interests.

He seemed set to tackle the issues of the day and to draw the publicity that went along with his fame. But the sailing was not to be as smooth for the old sailor as it looked on that day.

NOTES

1. John Corry, "Honor, Duty and a War Called Vietnam on CBS," *New York Times*, April 25, 1985, http://query.nytimes.com/gst/fullpage.html?res=940CE0D E1F38F936A15757C0A963948260.

2. John McCain with Mark Salter, *Worth the Fighting For* (New York: Random House, 2002), p. 113.

3. Paul Alexander, *Man of the People: The Life of John McCain* (Hoboken, NJ: Wiley, 2005), p. 105.

4. Dan Nowicki and Bill Muller, "The Senate Calls," *Arizona Republic*, March 1, 2007, p. 1.

5. Ibid.

6. George Will, "Hanoi to Phoenix to Washington," *Washington Post*, February 20, 1986, p. A17.

7. Robert Timberg, *John McCain: An American Odyssey* (New York: Free Press, 1999), p. 169.

8. Phil Duncan and the CQ Political Staff, *Congressional Quarterly's Politics in America 1988, the 100th Congress*. Washington, DC: CQ Press, 1987.

9. R. W. Apple Jr., "National Role Is Seen for Arizona Nominee," *New York Times*, November 2, 1986, http://query.nytimes.com/gst/fullpage.html?res=9A0D E0DF113FF931A35752C1A960948260.

Chapter 11

LOYALTY AND POLITICS

McCain, now 51 years old, began his life as a new senator just as he had done almost everything else in his political career—in a hurry. He took his committee assignments seriously and delighted in questioning witnesses himself. When once he had fed questions to other senators, now he was the one asking them.

And he didn't give any quarter to any witness—friend or foe. Years later, when his old friend Bill Cohen was nominated and then confirmed as Defense Secretary (in 1997, under President Bill Clinton), McCain was often the one to fire tough questions at him about national security policy.

"The test of John's character is that he never cut me any slack as Secretary of Defense," Cohen said.[1]

In his first term in the Senate, McCain ran, unsuccessfully, for a Republican leadership post, chairman of the Republican Senatorial Campaign Committee, the panel that recruits, finances, and helps Republican Senate candidates. While he was disappointed at the loss, he kept up his hard-charging work ethic in the Senate.

He came to the attention of Vice President George H. W. Bush, who was by this time running for president to succeed Ronald Reagan. His name was bandied about as a possible vice presidential choice, though McCain never got any official entreaties on the subject. He was asked to give a speech at the Republican national convention in 1988 in New Orleans. Nervously, he prepared for the speech. It was fine, but it was completely overshadowed by Reagan's valedictory "shining city on a hill" speech that roused the convention to its feet in tribute.[2]

McCain didn't get to be vice president. Instead, Bush selected Senator Dan Quayle of Indiana, a young, inexperienced senator. Quickly, press investigations of Quayle found that he had evaded the draft during the Vietnam War by pulling strings to get into the Indiana National Guard. It was not a rare tactic in those days, when influential people attempted to avoid combat by many means. Nonetheless, Quayle's tactics would prove difficult for Bush.

The press was swirling around New Orleans as the Quayle story broke, only hours after his announcement. McCain was asked if Quayle's National Guard service was a problem. He replied, "Well, only if he did get special favors to help him evade the draft." That was not exactly what the Bush team wanted to hear from its most famous veteran of the Vietnam War, but it was the truth, and everyone had to live with it. The Quayle controversy never did go away, but Bush was elected anyway and became the forty-first president of the United States.[3]

Bush decided to appoint former Senator John Tower, a Republican of Texas, as his Secretary of Defense. McCain was thrilled for his old friend, from whom he had learned so much about international relations and military affairs during their many trips abroad when McCain was Navy Senate liaison. He could see no more qualified a person than Tower for the job, and he looked forward to helping Tower through the Senate confirmation hearings, which he assumed would be no problem given Tower's experience and knowledge.

How wrong he turned out to be.

McCain knew full well that Tower liked to drink. He recalled his days of getting liquor for Tower on congressional trips abroad and their fun times going out after official meetings. "He worked hard and liked to relax at the end of the day with a glass or two or even three of Johnnie Walker Black," McCain said.[4] But others recalled the incidents in a much more sinister way.

Rumors began to spread about Tower's behavior. Even as the nomination was announced, there was talk of drinking and womanizing by the married Tower. He denied wrongdoing, but the charges prompted an extra FBI investigation. That, in and of itself, was spelling trouble for Tower.

The investigation rebutted the charges one at a time. But, in some ways, it served to further expose the charges and made it difficult for senators to vote for him. A summary of the charges and rebuttals was made public, including a charge that he seduced a woman at a party (the woman said he was helping her to the bathroom); that he had an affair with a Russian ballerina (no ballerina was ever found); that a businessman said he observed Tower drunk at a Washington hotel (Tower was out of the country at the time); that another businessman said he was drunk at a party in West Germany (other witnesses did not corroborate the story); and that Tower was alleged to be drunk at the Monocle, a popular Capitol Hill restaurant (waiters did not corroborate the story).[5]

Opponents of the nomination made the case that Tower's behavior could pose a security risk to the nation. They were concerned that if a crisis occurred when Tower was drinking, he would not be able to handle it. There was another aspect to the charges, as well. The times were changing. Behavior that was once accepted on Capitol Hill—convivial drinking many nights—was falling out of favor. Members of the Senate were concerned about perceptions of impropriety, as well as the impropriety itself. And Tower, never an easy man to get along with, had enemies. He had been particularly tart with Senator Sam Nunn, a Democrat of Georgia, when Tower had chaired the Senate Armed Services Committee. Now Nunn, a smart, straitlaced individual, headed the committee. He wasn't Tower's ally.

All of this was devastating for McCain, who viewed Tower as something of a father figure, as well as a mentor and teacher. McCain dug in to try to save the nomination. He collaborated with White House aides to try to play the public relations game to save Tower. He talked to his fellow senators to try to point out Tower's qualifications and knowledge. And he argued, sometimes vociferously, with Tower's opponents, asking them where the evidence of disqualification was coming from and whether it was even true.

"I continued to browbeat, chastise, and try to shame members into supporting Tower," McCain wrote.[6]

Politics was also coming into play in the Tower nomination. In the powerful post of chairman of the Armed Services Committee, Nunn had made the vote on Tower a test of loyalty for his fellow Democrats. Some lacked the seniority to buck the chairman. Some were simply disinclined to upset the powerful chairman. The committee voted 11–9 against Tower but allowed the nomination to go to the full Senate. However, his fate was sealed at that point.

The Senate debate took several days—excruciating days for Tower and McCain. When McCain rose to speak on the Senate floor about the Tower nomination, he knew what the outcome would be. But he mounted an eloquent and passionate defense of his friend.

"Ernest Hemingway defined courage as grace under pressure. No Cabinet nominee has ever faced as much pressure as John Tower has faced, pressure which has been ill founded, ill conceived, perhaps ill intentioned and unfair. No man has ever handled such unfairness, such

personal attacks, such pressure with as much grace as John Tower," Mc-
Cain said. "The country has lost the service of a man without peer in his
ability to perform that job and make this Nation more secure in a physically sound manner. The Senate has also lost. It has lost its fairness, its
respect for propriety, and its bipartisanship on defense issues. It has lost
its sense of historical precedent, and it has lost its institutional humility,
confusing the issue of whether it has the power to veto a nominee and
whether it should exercise that power."

Then McCain told a story of visiting a Naval installation with Tower,
who, as a former enlisted man, always went to visit the chief petty officer,
a high-ranking enlisted man, at whatever institution they were at. At the
end of the visit, the officer came over to Tower and shook his hand, saying
"God bless you, John Tower, you are a damned fine sailor."[7]

McCain repeated the quote, near tears. The Senate rejected the Tower
nomination anyway, 53–47. Tower died in a plane crash in 1991, on his
way to a party to celebrate publication of his book about the rejected
nomination, *Consequences: A Personal and Political Memoir.*

The Tower affair taught McCain a valuable lesson about perception,
politics, and how someone's career can be destroyed. He would need all of
that new knowledge in his next fight—self-described as the most difficult
of his political life.

NOTES

1. William S. Cohen, interview with author, Bethesda, Maryland, July 9, 2008.

2. Ronald Reagan, Remarks to 1988 Republican National Convention, August 15, 1988, New Orleans, Louisiana. The Heritage Foundation collection,
http://www.reagansheritage.org/html/reagan_rnc_88.shtml.

3. John McCain with Mark Salter, *Worth the Fighting For* (New York: Random
House, 2002), pp. 123–24.

4. Ibid., p. 129.

5. Bernard Weinraub, "White House Outlines Drive to Save Tower Nomination," *New York Times,* February 26, 1989, http://query.nytimes.com/gst/fullpage.
html?res=950DEED8173CF935A15751C0A96F948260&sec=&spon=&page
wanted=all.

6. McCain, *Worth the Fighting For,* p. 155.

7. *Congressional Record,* March 9, 1989, p. S2443.

John Sidney McCain III is held by his grandfather, John Sidney McCain, Sr., and accompanied by his father, John Sidney McCain, Jr., at his christening at Coco Solo, Panama Canal Zone, in 1936. Family photo, courtesy of Joe McCain.

John McCain, age 17 (fourth from right), joined his family at the launching of the first USS McCain, in Bath, Maine, in 1952. His mother, Roberta, is at John's right, with his father looking over her shoulder. At the luncheon after the launching, Admiral William Halsey, the featured speaker, would ask John if he drank liquor. Eyeing his mother, John said "no," but Halsey brought him a bourbon and water anyway, in honor of his grandfather. Family photo, courtesy of Joe McCain.

John McCain poses with his father, both wearing formal dress Navy uniforms, as a Naval Academy cadet. Family photo, courtesy of Joe McCain.

John McCain wed Carol Shepp in July 1965. In this wedding photograph, they are flanked by Roberta McCain (left), John McCain, Jr., and Joe McCain. Family photo, courtesy of Joe McCain.

McCain is pulled from Truc Bach Lake in Hanoi after being shot down over North Vietnam in October 1967. Courtesy of Library of Congress.

After his release from a North Vietnamese prison in 1973, McCain met President Richard M. Nixon. Family photo, courtesy of Joe McCain.

John McCain, with Cindy McCain and their two oldest children, Meghan and Jack, returned to Bath, Maine, in 1994 for the launching of the second USS McCain. U.S. Navy photo, courtesy of Joe McCain.

Senator John McCain walks with President Ronald W. Reagan in the West Wing colonnade of the White House in this publicity photo taken in 1987. Courtesy of Library of Congress.

John McCain poses with his son Jack, then a Naval Academy plebe, in 2005. Family photo, courtesy of Joe McCain.

John McCain campaigns for president at the U.S. Naval Academy in Annapolis, 2008. Courtesy of Elaine S. Povich.

Chapter 12

THE KEATING FIVE SCANDAL

In the fall of 1989, McCain's press secretary, Torie Clarke, was starting to roast a pig on the small patio of her Washington, DC, apartment. McCain's foreign policy assistant (and later co-author of his books), Mark Salter, was dousing the pig with lighter fluid in an attempt to get the meat to catch fire, when Clarke's phone rang. It was her boss, John McCain, who sounded uncharacteristically depressed.

McCain apologized for not attending the party, saying that he felt he might be a "wet blanket." Clarke remonstrated with him that he could never be that, even in his darkest days.[1]

But it turned out that McCain's comment about his mood was all too correct. The scandal that had him so subdued would come to be known as the "Keating Five," and it would affect him for the rest of his career.

McCain's association with Phoenix land developer Charles Keating began in 1981, when McCain was setting down his roots in Arizona. The two met at a Navy League dinner where McCain spoke, and they became friends. Their families socialized; their wives liked each other. In McCain's 1982 run for the House, Keating raised money for him, collecting more than $11,000 from employees at his company, American Continental Corporation. That was a lot of money in those days, and the two cemented their friendship. Keating helped out in McCain's run for House re-election in 1984, too, and when McCain ran for the Senate, Keating was there to host fundraising dinners and collect more money.[2]

They both had been fighter pilots, and Keating hosted the McCains at his vacation home in the Bahamas. Later, the Internal Revenue Service questioned whether the McCains had reimbursed Keating for the flights.

McCain said he thought his wife had repaid the money, but she hadn't, and they sent American Continental $13,000.

Keating's wealth came from American Continental and from an expanding interest in the booming savings and loan business. In the 1980s the U.S. government was loosening up regulations on savings and loans, trying to encourage them to branch out from their core businesses of administering savings accounts and making home mortgage loans. But the new rules that were designed to enhance savings and loans led to their self-destruction. The savings and loans invested in speculative ventures that many times weren't profitable. By 1983, more than a third of the S&Ls weren't profitable, and nine percent were bankrupt. Eventually, the government had to step in and bail them out, costing the taxpayers more than $120 billion.

Keating's savings and loan venture turned out to be the most expensive failure. In the early 1980s, he had purchased Lincoln Savings and Loan in Irvine, California, and was busy building that business. Federal investigators would find years later that he had engaged in questionable business practices, but that was not apparent when McCain first knew him.[3]

In March 1986, the Federal Home Loan Bank Board, the federal regulatory agency that oversees savings and loan institutions, was investigating Lincoln's investment practices. Keating was trying to get the bank board to go easy on him. It wasn't working. So he decided to enlist political help.

He had been a large political donor for years. His gifts to McCain were small compared to some of his other giving. He was once asked if he expected favors in return for his help. He was unequivocal. "I want to say in the most forceful way I can: I certainly hope so," he said.[4]

Keating engineered two meetings in 1987 with members of the U.S. Senate: Democrats Alan Cranston of California, Don Riegle of Michigan, John Glenn of Ohio, and Dennis DeConcini, McCain's fellow Arizonan, and McCain, the only Republican. All had a relationship with Keating, and all had gotten campaign contributions from the wealthy savings and loan man. Now Keating was stuck, and he wanted a return on his investment in the form of help from the senators.

DeConcini took the lead in helping Keating. DeConcini at first asked McCain to fly to San Francisco with him and talk to the regulators, but McCain said no.

On March 24, Keating went to DeConcini's office in Washington, where he was now trying to speak with regulators, and asked him if the meeting with regulators was going to happen. DeConcini reported that McCain was apprehensive about the proposed meeting. "Ah, McCain's a wimp," Keating said, indicating he would meet with McCain later.[5]

Anyone who knew McCain knew that he didn't like to have his courage questioned, under any circumstances. If Keating was trying to get under McCain's skin, he succeeded. McCain agreed to have the meeting, but his relationship with Keating was irrevocably broken. At the session, McCain lashed out at Keating, "Charlie I am not a coward, and I didn't spend five and a half years in a Vietnamese prison so that you could question my courage or my integrity," he said.[6] But Keating had accomplished at least a bit of what he wanted.

While McCain refused to negotiate a deal with Ed Gray, head of the Home Loan Bank Board, on Keating's behalf, he did agree to ask why the investigation had taken so long. Keating and American Continental and, by derivation, Lincoln Savings and Loan were, in fact, big employers in Arizona, and McCain felt he owed it to his constituents to at least pose a question to federal regulators.

Two meetings then occurred that were the focus of all the attention that was to come and all the consternation for McCain. The first, on April 2, included McCain, Cranston, Glenn, and Ed Gray of the Federal Home Loan Bank Board. According to McCain, he asked Gray if the meeting was improper, and Gray said it was okay to ask questions. The senators asked about the investigation of Lincoln and what was taking so long. They didn't get much in the way of answers, because Gray was constrained in what he could say about an ongoing investigation. Gray suggested to the senators that they meet with the local regulators from San Francisco, who had closer jurisdiction over Lincoln Savings and Loan because it was based in California.

On April 9, McCain, Glenn, DeConcini, and Riegle met with the San Francisco regulators in Washington. Cranston showed up very briefly, as he was busy handling legislation on the Senate floor. The regulators, according to what they told the Senate Ethics Committee later, felt intimidated by the senators. They felt the senators were trying to get them to drop their investigation of Lincoln Savings and Loan. One of them finally told the senators that they would be sending a "criminal referral" to the Justice Department about Lincoln, the first step toward an indictment.[7]

The investigation of Lincoln Savings and Loan dragged on. Finally, on April 12, 1989, American Continental filed for bankruptcy protection, and the next day the government took control of Lincoln. Investors lost millions, and the government spent $1.3 billion bailing out Lincoln.[8]

Newspapers started to pick up on the story, framing it that the five senators had taken $1.3 million in campaign contributions (most of which went to Cranston) to try to protect one of the worst savings and loan failures ever. The *Arizona Republic* started to sniff around McCain.

McCain's stock answer had been that he was merely trying to help out a constituent that did a lot of business in his state. But then the *Republic* revealed the extent of their relationship—the airplane trips to the Bahamas (that weren't reimbursed until after the fact) were just the beginning. The newspaper reported, on October 8, 1989, that Cindy McCain and her father, Jim Hensley, had invested $359,100 in a Keating shopping center in April 1986. This was the story that McCain had worried about in his conversation with his press secretary, Torie Clarke.

He had good reason to worry, because, unknown to Clarke, McCain had had a conversation with the *Republic* reporter before the story ran and had completely lost his temper.

"You're a liar," McCain said when a *Republic* reporter asked him about the business relationship between his wife and Keating.

"That's the spouse's involvement, you idiot," McCain said later in the same conversation. "You do understand English, don't you?"

He also belittled reporters when they asked about his wife's ties to Keating.

"It's up to you to find that out, kids."

"Even the Vietnamese didn't question my ethics," McCain added.[9]

The "kids" at the *Arizona Republic* found out everything. And they printed it.

When the story broke, Clarke and McCain went into crisis mode. McCain knew he was in big trouble because of the perception involved. There were echoes of John Tower's situation running through his head. He had to do something. Yes, he went to two meetings on Keating's behalf, but he hadn't done nearly as much to pressure the regulators as the other senators, and he needed to get that story out. Yes, he once had a relationship with Keating, but that was over.

"It happened so quickly and with such force," Clarke said. "Everyone realized it was bad. McCain realized the enormity of it more than anybody else. We were all saying, 'this isn't good,' he was saying, 'this is really bad, this is the worst thing that's ever happened in my career.'"[10]

McCain decided he would go the press and tell his side of the story. That decision was controversial. Some of his aides told him he should just lay low, get on with his business, and the story would go away. But he didn't think so. He decided to go to Arizona and have a press conference and talk about the Keating situation for as long as any member of the media wanted to ask him questions.

Clarke was in agreement with the strategy, but she had a concern. McCain's temper, which already had gotten him in trouble on this story, might surface again. The two devised a signaling system. If McCain started to get angry, Clarke, sitting in the front row, would rub her nose with her forefinger, warning him to calm down.

McCain took questions for 90 minutes. "I freely admit my errors," he said.[11] Clarke never did have to rub her nose.[12]

He then began a media blitz both in Arizona and in Washington. He met with every newspaper editorial board that would have him. The editorial boards write the editorials in newspapers and often have great influence. He talked to every reporter who called there as well. He put Arizona reporters first, then national reporters or reporters from other states. He played the time zone game, beginning calls early in the morning with East Coast reporters and often calling late into the night to make West Coast deadlines.

Some worried that he was talking too much, and there was always the possibility that he would explode again. But the tactic seemed to be working. One editorial board gave him credit for making a clean breast of things. One town in Arizona gave him a testimonial. Roger Mudd, a reporter on Public Television's *MacNeil/Lehrer NewsHour*, called McCain's open-door policy a "roll of the dice."[13]

Once back in Washington, McCain decided he would take questions about the Keating mess from any reporter who called. Aides were instructed to take calls from reporters, and McCain would call them back. McCain's tactics upset some of his fellow members of the Keating Five, who had decided to go to ground and hope that the story would fade. But the decision to talk was paying some dividends for McCain, however slight. He went on television; he was written about in major newspapers like the *New York Times* and *The Wall Street Journal*.

"I should stop talking about it," he told *Times* reporter Susan Rasky after a grueling 16-hour hour day spent in Arizona talking about it. "I am going to stop talking about it."

But his speaking schedule for the next day showed another round of appearances in the northern part of the state. "It's like a campaign," he told Rasky, with a smile, one of the few he had managed since the scandal broke. "A campaign for credibility."[14]

McCain's romancing of the press foreshadowed his behavior in campaigns in the coming years. From that point on, he was always very solicitous of reporters, joking with them and flattering them with access to him and to his campaigns. The technique would come into full bloom in his first race for the presidency in 2000, when he referred to reporters as "my base" and invited them to spend hours interviewing him on his bus, which he dubbed the "Straight Talk Express."

But, in 1989, all he wanted to do was survive and keep his Senate seat.

ETHICS INVESTIGATION

In addition to whatever political fallout McCain was experiencing at home and in the press, the political situation in Washington was worse. The Senate Ethics Committee was starting to get involved in the Keating Five issue and undertook an investigation of improprieties in the case. For months, McCain worried about what the committee would do, but he could do virtually nothing to influence it, lest he be accused of improperly intervening.

The House Banking Committee, which had no jurisdiction over McCain and the others, nonetheless held hearings on the Keating Five affair, which served to fuel the public fire around the scandal.

In November, the Senate Ethics Committee announced that it had hired Robert Bennett, a well-known Washington lawyer, to conduct an investigation into the Keating Five. Bennett was known for being fair and thorough, and his selection promised a long ordeal no matter what the outcome.

All of the Keating Five hired their own lawyers. McCain hired John Dowd, a well-known Washington attorney, whom he credited with helping him survive the experience. Each of the members of the Keating Five prepared written reports for the committee. McCain's ran 96 pages. After the reports were delivered to the committee, all McCain and the others could do was wait. The waiting proved awful for McCain. He really wanted the situation to be over with, but it would take months. He continued to keep up his contacts with the press and civic groups in Arizona.

In March and April of 1990, the Ethics Committee took depositions from the five senators. Then-Senator Warren Rudman, a New Hampshire Republican and a member of the Ethics Committee at the time, wrote in his own memoir of the moving scene when McCain, with tears in his eyes, said he would never do anything to dishonor the Senate or his family's long tradition of public service.[15]

Rudman and many others thought that McCain and Glenn had been unfairly wrapped up in the Keating Five along with the other three senators. Rudman thought Glenn and McCain were, if not innocent, guilty of far less serious offenses than their peers. Rudman thought the case against the two should be dropped. Bennett agreed. He recommended that Glenn and McCain not be punished at all.

But politics was never far away, and McCain was the only Republican in the group. If Glenn and McCain were dropped, the scandal was going to land only on Democrats, and midterm elections were coming up. Democrats didn't want to allow the scandal to be only a Democratic problem. Then there was the issue of public hearings. The public, understandably upset about the savings and loan crisis, wanted public hearings. The pressure was immense. In the end, the Senate Ethics Committee agreed to the hearings.

The hearings were excruciating for McCain. He hated testifying and telling the same stories over and over in public. He hated having Cindy's oversight in not paying the airplane bill exposed. But he did it, sitting through day after day of hearings. The hearings finally ended on January 16, 1991, nearly four years after the meetings with Charles Keating had taken place.

The committee deliberations took more time, particularly because members had to sort out how much punishment to dole out to each of the senators. In the end, the panel reprimanded McCain and Glenn for "poor judgment." That was it. The other three got harsher punishments. Riegle's actions "gave the appearance of being improper." DeConcini's conduct was "inappropriate." Cranston got the harshest punishment—a committee reprimand that was filed on the Senate floor. There was never a Senate vote on any of them.

"Senator McCain has violated no law of the United States or specific Rule of the United States Senate; therefore, the committee concludes that no further action is warranted," the committee wrote.[16]

Later, after a reasonable amount of time had passed and McCain thought it was appropriate to talk to Rudman about the case, McCain was still despondent. "He said, 'What I've been through with this is worse than being in a North Vietnamese prison,'" Rudman recalled. "I don't think most of us have any idea of how he views honor and fealty and loyalty. To him his honor being totally challenged and him accused of being a dishonest human being was worse than any punishment or torture as POW."[17]

McCain was relieved that the Keating Five episode was, at last, ended. But it would not be complete for him until he faced the voters another time. His popularity, as measured by polls, had dropped precipitously. The authoritative *Almanac of American Politics* thought he was washed up, at least nationally. "He is obviously finished as a vice presidential possibility, nor is he likely to emerge as a major national Republican spokesman and he has lost some of the saintly reputation he had."[18]

What they hadn't counted on was McCain's extraordinary resilience and ability to put the bad things behind him and move on. He was about to throw himself into the Senate, politics, and issues as he never had before.

NOTES

1. Torie Clarke, *Lipstick on a Pig: Winning in the No Spin Era by Someone Who Knows the Game* (New York: Free Press, 2006), pp. 3–4.

2. Dan Nowicki and Bill Muller, "McCain Profile: Chapter 7: The Keating Five Scandal," *Arizona Republic,* March 1, 2007, http://www.azcentral.com/news/specials/mccain/articles/0301mccainbio-chapter7.html.

3. Warren Rudman, *Combat: Twelve Years in the U.S. Senate* (New York: Random House, 1996), p. 206.

4. Jerry Kammer, "Keating: Shattered Myth Plea Ends Chapter in S&L Scandal," *Arizona Republic,* April 11, 1999, p. A1.

5. John McCain with Mark Salter, *Worth the Fighting For* (New York: Random House, 2002), p. 174.

6. Ibid., p. 175.

7. Rudman, *Combat,* p. 213.

8. Ibid., p. 216.

9. Nowicki and Muller, "McCain Profile: Chapter 7: The Keating Five Scandal."

10. Torie Clarke, interview with author, Bethesda, Maryland, July 8, 2008.

11. Michael Kranish, "Five Senators Who Aided S & L Face Queries on Contributors," *Boston Globe*, October 18, 1989, p. 1.

12. Torie Clarke, *Lipstick on a Pig,* p. 5.

13. Ibid., p. 7.

14. Susan F. Rasky, "Washington Talk: To Senator McCain, the Savings and Loan Affair Is Now a Personal Demon," *New York Times,* December 22, 1989, http://query.nytimes.com/gst/fullpage.html?res=950DE6DF1031F931A15751C1A96F948260&sec=&spon=&pagewanted=all.

15. Rudman, Combat, p. 218.

16. "Excerpts of Statement by Senate Ethics Panel," *New York Times,* February 28, 1991, http://query.nytimes.com/gst/fullpage.html?res=9D0CE2D71539F93BA15751C0A967958260&sec=&spon=&pagewanted=all.

17. Warren Rudman, interview with author, Washington, DC, August 1, 2008.

18. Michael Barone and Grant Ujifusa, *The Almanac of American Politics 1992. National Journal* (Washington, DC, 1991).

Chapter 13

REGAINING HIS REPUTATION

McCain began his political resurrection on two fronts—securing his own re-election and engaging in frequent news-making commentary. On the political front, he continued to throw himself into his 1992 re-election bid. But again, it was not a good year for Republicans. Anti-incumbent fever was sweeping the nation, led by nose-diving approval ratings for President George H. W. Bush. The savings and loan scandal—in which the Keating Five and McCain were wrapped up—was helping to fuel the fire against current officeholders.

This election year, 1992, was also dubbed the "Year of the Woman," and McCain had drawn a female opponent in his election race that was heating up in 1991. The Democrat running against him was Phoenix community activist Claire Sargent. The election was also complicated by the independent candidacy of former Governor Evan Mecham. Mecham had been indicted on six felony counts back in 1988, and McCain had denounced him. Mecham's candidacy seemed aimed at payback for what he viewed as McCain's "disloyalty."

McCain had plenty of money for his re-election campaign, while Sargent and Mecham had little. McCain used his funds to blanket the state with advertising. Those ads didn't mention the Keating Five at all. Rather, they touted his record on the environment, Hispanic and American Indian issues, and the elderly.[1]

Elderly voters, a growing part of the Arizona population, were a particular target for McCain, since he had led the fight to repeal the so-called Medicare catastrophic health insurance law. Congress had enacted the law only a year earlier. It was designed to protect elderly people who became seriously ill. It covered expensive treatments, and it put a small surtax on elderly people to pay for it. Lawmakers thought they were doing the right thing for older Americans, but the older people rebelled at the extra tax and criticized the law for failing to cover nursing home stays. They started demonstrations and petition drives to get rid of the law. In one memorable scene, former Representative Dan Rostenkowski, a Chicago Democrat and author of the catastrophic law, had his car chased down the street by an angry mob of old folks who wouldn't get out of the way as they shouted at him.

McCain didn't have to fight off angry old people, but Congress as a whole and McCain individually decided to do something. McCain took the lead in getting rid of the program that had the elderly so up in arms.

On the day it was repealed, McCain called the action a "victory for the nation's seniors."[2]

During the campaign, McCain's opponents would criticize him for taking too much credit for repealing the law, but the facts showed that he did take the lead and worked hard to negotiate a compromise between the House and the Senate on the issue. The negotiation was made more difficult by the fact that many in Congress were proud of the law they had enacted just the year before and really didn't want to get rid of it. But they bowed to political reality and the voting power of senior citizens in repealing the law.

In addition to tending to health care issues, McCain became a champion of smaller, start-up airlines like Arizona's America West by urging the opening up of flying slots at crowded airports such as New York's LaGuardia and John F. Kennedy airports, Washington's National Airport, and Chicago's O'Hare.

In another important area, he continued his support for Native Americans, helping to push through Congress the Indian Child Abuse Prevention and Treatment Act.

On the international front, McCain also was much in demand as a commentator because of his military experience, particularly during the 1991 Gulf War. The Gulf War was fought when Iraq, in a dispute with neighboring Kuwait over oil, invaded Kuwait. The United States and the United Kingdom put together a coalition of 34 nations to repulse the Iraqis. The war was fought in January and February 1991, a very brief time for a war. Iraqis fought back by launching missiles into Saudi Arabia and Israel. But the coalition kept pushing the Iraqi troops back into Iraq and toward the capital of Baghdad. The war ended when the coalition troops chased the invading Iraqis and the Iraqis gave up. Kuwait celebrated.[3]

The war was a very intense period in American history, and most Americans were tuned to radio, television, and the Internet more than usual to get the latest war news. Television, in particular, played a big role, as the invading troops were accompanied by reporters who, for the first time in modern warfare, sent back live pictures of the war in progress.

Because 24-hour news channels by definition never sleep, they needed expert commentary frequently. McCain, because of his previous war experience, was happy to appear and to lend his expertise to the conversation about the war. Particularly when Americans were taken prisoner, McCain's experiences resonated with the American people. And, when McCain was talking about the Gulf War, he wasn't talking about the Keating Five.

McCain was also cementing his reputation as a media-friendly senator. He joked with makeup people in the studios; he was respectful and solicitous of reporters. Talk shows liked having him on, because he answered questions knowledgeably and thoroughly.

"The Today Show called and we started on the Today Show at four-something in the morning," former McCain aide Scott Celley told the *Arizona Republic*. "The last thing I remember him being on was Australian Nightline, which was done here at Channel 10, a few blocks away, at close to 11 P.M. He was on television or the radio every minute of that day."[4]

In the end, the re-election race wasn't close. McCain got 56 percent of the vote in the three-way contest, which saw Mecham finish last. The Keating Five issue never really surfaced.

"The pictures of me cavorting on a Bahamian beach with Charlie that I had anticipated seeing in Arizona newspapers never made an appearance in the campaign," McCain wrote later.[5]

Of the Keating Five, three (DeConcini, Cranston, and Riegle) retired. Glenn was re-elected.

CINDY'S ORPHAN AND CINDY'S PAIN

While McCain fought the battle of the Keating Five and burnished his reputation as an international commentator, his wife was raising a family and doing charity work. At the end of the Gulf War, Cindy McCain camped in the Kuwait desert to take medical supplies to refugees as part of her charity, the American Voluntary Medical Team. Later in 1991, she visited Mother Teresa's orphanage in Bangladesh, also as part of her medical team work. There, she found many babies who had been abandoned, including one with a cleft palate so severe she could barely be fed. Another baby had a bad heart defect. Cindy McCain worried that the two babies wouldn't survive in the orphanage, so she applied for visas to take them to the United States. But Bangladeshi officials became incensed at the idea that they couldn't take care of their own babies and refused to sign the paperwork at the airport to allow them to leave. "We can do surgery on this child," an official said. Cindy, usually a mild-mannered woman and unfailingly polite, got mad. "Then do it," she shouted, risking arrest by airport authorities. "What are you waiting for?" The official, taken aback, signed the papers.[6]

Cindy met her husband at the airport, carrying the baby with the cleft palate. John asked her, quietly, "Where's she going?" Cindy replied, "To our house." McCain just laughed and said, "I thought so." Cindy McCain brought home a baby without telling her husband, and he just accepted it, a fact that she found remarkable but not unexpected.[7]

But Cindy was fighting a demon, as well. During the time of the Keating scandal, she had several surgeries on her back for a ruptured disc that she initially suffered while lifting her son, Jimmy, when he was small. She got pain pills for her back problems. But when the Keating story broke, particularly the part about her forgetting to reimburse Keating for the flights to the Bahamas, she began taking more than the prescribed dose. She got prescriptions, initially. But, as her habit intensified, she began filching pills from her own charity.[8]

Finally, her mother noticed that something was wrong. McCain, busy repairing his own reputation, was oblivious. Cindy told her mother what was going on and quit the pills. She went into rehabilitation. But the episode didn't end there. An employee who had been fired from her charity organization called the Drug Enforcement Administration and reported the missing pills. Cindy, who had not told her husband anything, was forced to tell him the truth. He was sympathetic, but the troubles didn't end.

Newspapers were beginning to look into the story, following the former charity employee's lead. The McCains devised a strategy designed to get favorable press coverage. They invited a select group of reporters to hear Cindy's story and to hear McCain's comments.

"I was stunned," McCain said at the time. "Naturally, I felt enormous sadness for Cindy and a certain sense of guilt that I hadn't detected it. I feel very sorry for what she went through, but I'm very proud she was able to come out of it. For her, it was like the Keating affair had been for me, a searing experience, and we both came out stronger. I think it has strengthened our marriage and our overall relationship." The *Phoenix Gazette* columnist who first reported McCain's "the longest I ever lived in one place was Hanoi" comment wrote about Cindy's addiction story, too. His column was headlined: "I'm Cindy, and I'm an addict."[9]

While most of the initial press coverage was favorable, some of the reporters who were not let in on the story at first began reporting more negative details. One story indicated that the McCains might have improperly adopted their Bangladeshi daughter, whom they had named Bridget. A separate investigation found that the adoption was by the book. A particularly hard-hitting political cartoon showed Cindy McCain shaking an orphan for drugs, which fell out of the child's pockets. The employee tried to blackmail the McCains for $250,000. That strategy led to more favorable press coverage for the McCains and may have allowed Cindy to escape with only rehabilitation as her punishment. But the stories and the cartoons had a severe impact on Cindy McCain. While her husband courted reporters, she would stay away from the press for years.

NOTES

1. John E. Yang, Kenneth J. Cooper, and Tom Kenworthy, "McCain Seems to Solidify Lead over Female Rival, Ex-Governor," *Washington Post*, October 11, 1992, p. A35.

2. Martin Tolchin, "Congress Rescinds Long-Term Care Act before Adjourning," *New York Times*, November 22, 1989, http://query.nytimes.com/gst/fullpage.html?res=950DEFDE1630F931A15752C1A96F948260&sec=&spon=&&scp=10&sq=catastrophic%20health%20insurance%20repeal%20compromise%20mccain&st=cse Bottom of Form.

3. *USA Today*, Gulf War timeline, http://www.usatoday.com/news/index/iraq/nirq050.htm.

4. Dan Nowicki and Bill Muller, "McCain Profile. Chapter 8: Overcoming Scandal, Moving On," *Arizona Republic*, March 1, 2007, http://www.azcentral.com/news/election/mccain/articles/2007/03/01/20070301mccainbio-chapter8.html.

5. John McCain with Mark Salter, *Worth the Fighting For* (New York: Random House, 2002), p. 204.

6. Tatiana Sorokko, "Cindy McCain: Myth vs. Reality," *Harper's Bazaar*, July 2007, http://www.harpersbazaar.com/print-this/cindy-mccain-0707.

7. Ibid.

8. Holly Bailey, "In Search of Cindy McCain," *Newsweek*, June 30, 2008, pp. 20–27.

9. Nowicki and Muller, "McCain Profile: Chapter 8: Overcoming Scandal, Moving On."

Chapter 14

VIETNAM REVISITED

John McCain was a prisoner of war in Vietnam, but he never allowed himself to be a prisoner of the war and its aftermath once he got home. For a time, he rarely talked about his experiences in Vietnam, preferring to concentrate on his new life. But he could not escape his history. Unlike many veterans of the Vietnam War era, he managed to balance his past experience and his future.

On no issue was that more clear than the United States's relationship to Vietnam right after the war as well as years later. McCain's views were always respected when it came to Vietnam; his words had weight, his decisions never taken lightly.

After that first trip back with Walter Cronkite on the 10-year anniversary of the end of America's involvement in the war, McCain kept up his interest. Over the years, he made many trips back to that Southeast Asian nation, once with his young son, Jack, whom he showed the prison in which he was held. Each trip was emotional, but never debilitating, for McCain.

Some people who were caught up in the Vietnam War had a harder time coping with the aftermath. There were severe cases of posttraumatic stress syndrome among combat veterans. And many of them never were able to get past what they felt was disrespect from their fellow Americans when they got home. The opposition to the war that many Americans felt spilled over to the returning veterans, who sometimes were accused of committing war crimes. There had been crimes committed during the war—including the infamous My Lai massacre in which Lieutenant William Calley ordered his soldiers to perform a "search and destroy" mission on the village in which 300 civilians were killed. Calley was convicted of murder.[1]

But, for the most part, the returning veterans fought the best war they could and were stunned by the reactions at home to their service. Some just didn't talk about their war experience and let their emotions simmer inside. Others became involved in organizations memorializing the POWs and those missing in action (MIAs) from the war. The emotions over the Vietnam War grew less raw over time, but, for those who lived through it, they never completely went away.

McCain began to see Vietnam in a different light. He thought that it would be better to establish relations with the former enemy than to continue to let the emotions surrounding that war fester. It was a huge emotional and practical leap for McCain: a man who had been held in captivity for years wanting to see his country and the one that tortured him get along.

In March 1988, he wrote an opinion column for the *Washington Post* newspaper in which he called for better ties with the old adversary. He suggested establishing a U.S. "interest section" in Vietnam, something that fell short of establishing true diplomatic ties and setting up an embassy but that might put the nations on a path to diplomacy.

"Overcoming the trauma of the war will be a slow process for Vietnam and the United States. Establishing interest sections would, however, catalyze a resolution of outstanding political and humanitarian issues," he wrote. "Thirteen years after the fall of Saigon, the time has come for increased efforts to resolve the legacies of the Vietnam War."[2]

He took a lot of criticism for that opinion, including a rebuttal from conservative Representative Robert Dornan, R-Calif., who said such a move would "reward" Vietnam, which still had barbed wire on its borders to keep its citizens from leaving, was still occupying Cambodia, and had failed to "provide a full accounting of American MIAs."[3]

The issue of the MIAs had been simmering for years, with distraught families leading the way. The nation of Vietnam didn't help the situation by being uncooperative much of the time. Some of the missing were reported to have been last seen in Laos or Cambodia, nearby countries in Southeast Asia, and those governments weren't cooperative, either.

McCain continued to make trips to Vietnam, including one significant visit in April 1991, when he was asked to return to Vietnam by the Communist leaders of the country to help them account for the 2,282 American MIAs still listed as "missing" after that war.

McCain had to take a circuitous route to get to Vietnam, because of the lack of diplomatic relations. The two countries did not have embassies on each other's soil, they did not trade with each other, and visits by citizens of one nation to the other were extremely rare.

McCain went first to Thailand to meet with U.S. officials and to get a passport for Vietnam. He met in Vietnam with Nguyen Co Thach, a Vietnamese official whom he had met previously in Washington to discuss the issue of the POW/MIAs. The two had gotten along well, and McCain hoped they could continue their personal relationship. But the complexity of the relationship between their countries made it difficult. The United States was thinking about trying to normalize relations, and McCain was ready, but there were many conditions before that could happen. Americans remembered that after the American involvement in the Vietnam War ended, North Vietnam had promised not to invade South Vietnam. But it did, and the country became one under Communist rule.

The discussions continued, and one week after McCain returned to the United States, Vietnam and the United States agreed to open in Hanoi a U.S. POW/MIA office to get started on figuring out the fate of the missing men.[4]

But it was only a first step, and the issue was still emotional. In July 1991, *Newsweek* magazine ran a cover story with a picture of three men who were identified as missing from the Vietnam War. The pictures were grainy, the men's faces obscured. But relatives felt they might be their missing men. The uproar started all over again.[5]

McCain doubted that the pictures showed missing Americans. "They looked a little too paunchy and a little too relaxed to remind me of any prisoner of war I had ever known, especially prisoners who would have been in their third decade of captivity," McCain wrote. "If they were POWs, the food really had gotten a hell of a lot better since I left."[6]

Because of his fame, families of the missing sought out McCain. "Senator, I know my dad is alive" was just an example of the statements made to McCain by the families of the missing, many years after the war.[7]

McCain sympathized with the families, and he wanted to bring closure to the situation, even if it meant that the men would never be found and could be officially declared dead. To that end, he sponsored legislation requiring the Department of Defense to begin declassifying information on POW/MIAs.

Even in the Senate, there were those who felt that there might still be Americans alive in Southeast Asia. One was Senator Bob Smith, a New Hampshire Republican, who had made the issue something of a mission for him. Smith persuaded Senate leaders to empanel a committee to look into the POW/MIA issue—the third panel since the end of the war. Senator John Kerry, D-Mass., a Vietnam veteran who would later run unsuccessfully for president, was named to chair the panel. Smith was vice chairman, and McCain was appointed to the group. Hearings began in late 1990 and would continue the controversy. But this time, records were a little easier to obtain from the Vietnamese, and more information was available. It seemed that the Vietnamese were finally coming around to the idea that if they wanted better relations with the United States, particularly as a trading partner, they needed to be a little more cooperative.

The panel's final report was issued on January 13, 1993, and concluded that, while members had hoped to find evidence of American prisoners living in Southeast Asia, it was not to be. "Unfortunately, our hopes have not been realized," the report read.

> This disappointment does not reflect a failure of the investigation, but rather a confrontation with reality. While the Committee has some evidence suggesting the possibility a POW may have survived to the present, and while some information remains yet to be investigated, there is, at this time, no compelling evidence that proves that any American remains alive in captivity in Southeast Asia.[8]

The POW/MIA report was the first step toward normalization of relations with Vietnam, but it would take a few more years for the effort to come to fruition. Meanwhile, McCain suffered criticism at the hands of some who thought he had "sold out." They accused him of being a "Manchurian Candidate," after a movie in which a former Korean POW is brainwashed into becoming an assassin. The accusation stung, but McCain remained dedicated to his course of action. The "Manchurian Candidate" charge would surface many more times in his political career, but the more it came up, the more McCain could brush it away.

After the 1992 presidential election, when George H. W. Bush had lost to Bill Clinton, McCain and Kerry tried to persuade the lame-duck president to end the trade embargo against Vietnam, but Bush declined. The issue would be left to Clinton.

Clinton had a difficult relationship with many Americans, particularly those in the military, because he did not serve in the war in Vietnam, though he was eligible. He went to graduate school and used other methods to stay out of the draft and away from Vietnam. His lack of service became controversial in his presidential election, but he won anyway, mostly because other issues, like a bad economy, dominated the contest. Clinton was not a favorite of McCain, but McCain respected the office of president and supported his Commander in Chief. He urged Clinton to lift the embargo.

McCain was quietly helping Clinton in other ways, as well. When Memorial Day rolled around, Clinton was worried about making the traditional appearance at the Vietnam Veterans Memorial in Washington. The black marble V-shaped memorial had become a lightning rod for protest about the Vietnam War, and Clinton's record of avoiding service in that war threatened to undermine his participation in the ceremony. McCain urged him to go. The role of Commander in Chief does not go away just because the president lacks a war record, he reasoned.

"I told the new president it was his duty to go to the Wall that Memorial Day, and I would publicly defend his decision to do so and if he wished, accompany him to the ceremony," McCain wrote later.[9] Clinton did not ask McCain to appear with him, and, while there were protests, Clinton weathered the event in pretty good shape. McCain, meanwhile, had gone back to Hanoi to work on the issue of ending the trade embargo.

But the Clinton administration still dithered on recognizing Vietnam and resuming trade. A year later, in January 1994, the Senate, led by McCain and John Kerry, voted 62–38 for a resolution urging lifting of the embargo. The resolution's strong vote showed that a large majority of the Senate and, by inference, the American people were in favor of trade with Vietnam, if for no other reason than to permit more Americans to go into the closed country and search for evidence of American remains.[10]

In closing the debate on the resolution, McCain had the last word:

> I urge my colleagues to support this amendment, to not be intimidated by political pressure from quarters that may never support better relations with our former adversary. I can speak with some authority to that question since I have suffered the full brunt of their opposition and survived. On this question, that has so long divided our country, the right course may not be the most politically expedient, but it is the right course nonetheless. Let us do the right thing. Let us take such steps that will best honor our commitments, protect our interests and advance our values. There is no dishonor in that.[11]

McCain wanted a normalization of relations with Vietnam. It took Clinton a while, but, by July 1995, he was ready to grant formal recognition to Vietnam and to resume trading. McCain witnessed the ceremony and was enveloped in a bear hug by the president. The action was not without controversy. Some veterans groups excoriated the president for the action. Clinton needed the Senate vote to bolster him, and he needed John McCain.

"He never carries a grudge," said former Senator William Cohen, McCain's good friend. "He has the ability to not look back. He led the effort to normalize relations with Vietnam. This would not have happened without John McCain."[12]

Two years later, McCain's fellow POW Douglas "Pete" Peterson, an Air Force captain who was shot down in 1966 and who spent six years in Vietnamese captivity and who later became a congressman from Florida, was named ambassador to Vietnam.

NOTES

1. Public Broadcasting System, "The American Experience," Vietnam Online, The My Lai Massacre, http://www.pbs.org/wgbh/amex/vietnam/trenches/my_lai.html.

2. John McCain, "It's Time for Better Ties with Vietnam; Thoughts of an Ex-POW Who's Now in the Senate," *Washington Post*, March 21, 1998, p. A11.

3. Robert K. Dornan, "The Vietnamese Don't Deserve the Boost," *Washington Post*, March 29, 1988, p. A23.

4. John McCain with Mark Salter, *Worth the Fighting For* (New York: Random House, 2002), p. 234.

5. "Hoping against Hope: A Generation after Vietnam, a Blurry Photograph Reopens the Mia Mystery That Has Left Families with Their Lives on Hold," *Newsweek*, July 29, 1992, http://www.newsweek.com/id/128359.

6. McCain, *Worth the Fighting For*, p. 241.

7. Ibid.

8. Senate Report 103–1, "POW/MIA'S, Report of the Select Committee on POW/MIA Affairs," U.S. Senate, January 13, 1993, http://www.fas.org/irp/congress/1993_rpt/pow-exec.html.

9. McCain, *Worth the Fighting For*, p. 259.

10. Steven Greenhouse, "Senate Urges End to U.S. Embargo against Vietnam," *New York Times*, January 28, 1994, http://query.nytimes.com/gst/fullpage.html?res=9A02E3DC1639F93BA15752C0A962958260&sec=&spon=&pagewanted=print.

11. *Congressional Record*, January 26, 1994, p. S136.

12. William Cohen, interview with author, Washington, DC, July 9, 2008.

Chapter 15

MAVERICK

Vietnam occupied only a small amount of McCain's time in the 1990s. During that decade, he was also branching out and developing a reputation for taking independent stands, particularly ones that tended to upset his fellow Republicans. The "maverick" politician was about to be born.

Coming off the Keating Five scandal, McCain began to take a close look at the effect of money in politics. Having taken a bunch of cash from Keating, he knew how that kind of relationship can make politicians more willing to help the donors. While the members of Congress might not always do what their donors asked, the cash generally got the donors' feet inside the congressional door.

McCain was also looking at "pork barrel" spending—pet projects promoted by individual members of Congress that the government was footing the bill for. Now, one senator's pork barrel project is another's "necessary civic project," so taking on senators over bringing back the bacon for their home states was not going to endear McCain to anyone.

In addition, McCain sometimes seemed to delight in attacking the little perks that members of Congress enjoyed but that the public found outrageous. No issue was more reflective of this than the special parking lot for high-ranking government officials—senators, House members, Supreme Court justices, and the heads of foreign embassies—right next to the terminal at Washington's National Airport. Washington is rare among major U.S. cities in that one of its major airports is just a 10-minute drive from the downtown business district and the U.S. Capitol. The convenience of that airport (and its special little parking lot gem) is treasured by Congress, as members fly home nearly every weekend. On Thursday nights, as

Congress is generally winding up business for the week, the popular phrase is that members are willing to cast a lot of votes quickly because you can "hear the jet engines revving up at National."

McCain took advantage of the perquisite, just like every other senator. But he noticed the angry stares of the traveling public as they wrestled their luggage to the terminal from far-off parking lots or struggled to make their flights by riding Metro subway trains. The VIP parking lot was emblematic of everything the public hated about Washington and Congress.

McCain decided to take on the idea of getting rid of that little perk—something that did endear him to his fellow senators. Somewhat naively, he thought they would all fall in line once they knew that their constituents were upset. He introduced an amendment to scrap the free parking as an add-on to a bill about bankruptcy that the Senate was debating in April 1994. He said a few words about doing something that would "make members of Congress just like the rest of our fellow citizens . . . the people I represent" and left the chamber.[1] He figured the vote would be a slam dunk.

McCain hadn't counted on Senator John "Jack" Danforth, a Missouri Republican so well known for his fairness and rectitude that he was dubbed "St. Jack." Danforth took the floor and chalked McCain's amendment up to nothing less than disrespect of the institution of the U.S. Senate. Senators, Danforth said, were not like everybody else. They worked long hours and then raced to their home states on the weekends to work some more. "Is it a luxury to have a place to park? What are you supposed to do, shoot in a pneumatic tube over to National Airport?" he said. Danforth said that the move was nothing more than caving in to cynicism about Washington. Senators, he said, were engaged in a noble profession, and pandering to those who would diminish it was beneath the Senate.[2]

There was not a little resentment of McCain in that statement, as well, for bringing the issue up to public scrutiny. In the end, the Senate voted 53–44 to keep the free parking. McCain lost the vote and won no friends inside the Senate, but outside, in the public arena, people were beginning to take notice.

PORK BARRELING AND "EARMARKS"

McCain soon began going after congressional spending, which had been a favorite target for years, but McCain brought it to new heights. He started sending out press releases about particular spending items that he thought were excessive or silly. He developed a "scroll down and click on the pig" spot on his Web site, which pointed to projects such as the "$50,000 demonstration project on kudzu as a noxious weed" or the $180,000 allocation for the National Center for Physical Acoustics to develop automated methods of "monitoring pest populations."[3]

Of course, each one of the projects had a congressional sponsor, and his public methods again did not win him any friends among his colleagues.

By 1998, McCain had reached the peak of his objections to so-called earmarks—spending that is slipped into a bill by one senator or House member without anyone else discussing it or holding hearings. An "emergency" spending bill passed late that year particularly incensed him, and he took to the Senate floor to list some of the things that he felt were outrageous. He had compiled a 52-page list of things that he objected to, including:

$250,000 to an Illinois firm to research caffeinated chewing gum

$750,000 for grasshopper research in Alaska

$1.1 million for manure handling and disposal in Starkville, Mississippi

$250,000 for a Hawaii Volcanoes Observatory

$250,000 for a lettuce geneticist in Salinas, California

$162,000 for research on peach tree short life in South Carolina

$200,000 for research on turkey carnovirus in Indiana

$64,000 for urban pest research in Georgia

$100,000 for Vidalia onion research in Georgia

An additional $2.5 million for the Office of Cosmetics and Color

"We are wasting the people's money when we fund these dubious proposals," McCain said. "We undermine the faith of our constituents—the taxpayers—when we continue the practice of earmarking and inappropriately designating funding for projects based on political interests rather than national priority and necessity. Unfortunately, that has occurred here. This bill is a shameful example of why the American public has become cynical and skeptical of government."[4]

But the bill passed anyway, and McCain continued his somewhat quixotic crusade.

Part of the problem, as McCain saw it, was that many items were contained in a single bill. The spending bill that he was so outraged over in 1998 was about 4,000 pages long. And the way the Constitution is written, the president was not allowed to pick out parts of bills to sign or veto. It was all or nothing. That meant, for instance, if a president wanted to sign a bill funding the armed services and one senator had slipped in a pork project, the president had to accept the pork in order to get the military spending.

Presidents for years had always wanted what they called the "line-item veto," which would allow them to single out items in bills for rejection. Congress, for years, had opposed the idea, because a little logrolling— you accept my project and I'll accept yours—is part of the way Congress works.

But public pressure also was mounting on Congress to allow the line-item veto, and McCain was at the center of that pressure. He first introduced a line-item veto bill in 1992, but the Congress rejected it. The highlight of the debate was an eight-hour speech by venerable Senator Robert C. Byrd, a West Virginia Democrat, who was an authority on Senate history as well as someone who had directed more than a billion dollars in federal spending to his impoverished state through his position on the Senate Appropriations Committee. All spending goes through Appropriations, and Byrd always made sure that West Virginia got plenty of it.

"One man's pork is another man's job," said Byrd.

Also in his speech, Byrd framed the issue as one of congressional power versus the executive branch and presidential power. Senators were always anxious about any threat to their power, and Byrd made sure they were anxious about this one.

"I intend to discuss nothing less than the evolution of American democracy," Byrd said in his oration, based on a 10-inch-thick document he had compiled on the line-item veto. In his speech, he outlined the history and growth of the origins of democracy from the reign of King Ethelbald of Wessex (in what is now the United Kingdom) in 858.[5]

The election of 1992 brought a new president, Bill Clinton, a Democrat, who also wanted a line-item veto. McCain kept up the drumbeat.

The midterm congressional elections also brought change. Republicans took over both the House and Senate majorities. Republicans had run on something called the "Contract with America," and one of the tenets of that contract was the line-item veto.

The time was ripe, particularly because of a burgeoning national debt, and McCain pounced. By the spring of 1996, both houses of Congress had approved the measure and Clinton had signed it into law, despite the same objections from Senator Byrd and others that it would prove unconstitutional.

In Senate debate, before the 69–31 vote in favor, McCain said that, by allowing the debt to grow so high, "it is Congress that has failed the

American people." He said that presidents have been able to hide behind the excuse that they were forced to sign bills with lots of waste in them since they couldn't just excise the waste and let rest of the bill stand.

"Under a line-item veto," he said, "no one can hide."[6]

That was true, but the law couldn't be hidden from the courts, either. It was immediately challenged by Byrd and others senators. Clinton used it a couple of times—once to excise some projects in New York. The state promptly also sued. Eventually, the line-item veto ended up in the Supreme Court, which ruled in 1998 that it was unconstitutional.

CAMPAIGN FINANCE REFORM

Meanwhile, McCain was attacking the system from another angle—an angle that would become his signature issue for the next decade—campaign finance reform.

For some time, McCain had been toying with the idea of changing the way campaigns were financed. But it was the election of Senator Russell Feingold, a Democrat from Wisconsin, that would prove to be the catalyst. McCain knew he needed a Democratic partner to get his ideas through the Senate, and Feingold seemed the ideal candidate. "He struck me as principled, independent and game, just the qualities I was looking for in a political ally who felt Congress was overdue for a little reform," McCain wrote.[7]

Feingold had been elected to the Senate in 1992 with a humorous campaign. In the Democratic primary, while the other two candidates battered each other with negative ads, Feingold ran clever, funny spots: one showing "Elvis Presley," long after the rock 'n' roll idol had died, alive and endorsing Feingold, another showing Feingold at home, opening up his closet door and saying, "Look, no skeletons!" While he campaigned on a three-point deficit reduction plan scratched on his garage door (the subject of another ad), the former Rhodes scholar backed up the "garage door" plan with an 82-point white paper.[8] He won the primary and went on to win the general election.

In the Senate, Feingold looked in some ways to be the opposite of McCain. He was liberal and voted against subsidized water for Western states like Arizona. In addition, he attacked defense spending and was opposed to the new CVN-76 aircraft carrier that McCain supported. But the two shared a reformist streak. They both worked on lobbying reform, for example. And then there was campaign finance.

The McCain-Feingold campaign finance bill was aimed at cutting down on spending by political candidates. The amount of money it takes to elect senators had grown every year, reaching many millions in some states with expensive media markets in big cities where buying television time is costly. Even in less populated states like Arizona and Wisconsin, elections were becoming prohibitively expensive. Specifically, the McCain-Feingold bill sought to banish "soft money," which was unregulated, unlimited money given by unions, corporations, and individuals to political parties, which would in turn be barred from giving the money to candidates.[9]

The two senators first introduced their bill in 1994, but it was filibustered to death by the Senate. They tried again several times without success.

It would take McCain's 2000 presidential campaign, the John F. Kennedy Profile in Courage Award for the two senators, and the Enron financial scandal, in which political donations played a part, for the bill to finally become law, in 2002. Faced with overwhelming support for change in the way campaigns were financed, President George W. Bush, who initially opposed the bill, finally signed it.

"What we've really done is take a couple hundred million Americans and give them an opportunity to be heard again in our nation's capital," McCain said.[10]

But opponents insisted that it would eventually be found unconstitutional. And the Supreme Court did pick out several parts of the law and throw them out several years later. But the central portion of the law—the ban on "soft money"—stayed.

For McCain, it cemented his role as a reformer and as someone willing to buck his own party.

He did it again in going after tobacco companies, which had always been defended by Republicans. But McCain, an ex-smoker, had been made chairman of the powerful Commerce Committee in the Senate, and he decided to wield that power to try to decrease the number of teenage smokers in the nation by increasing the tax on cigarettes so high that teens would not be able to afford to buy them. He proposed a $1.50-a-pack tax. The tobacco companies went ballistic. They mounted an advertising campaign tagging McCain as a tax-raiser. The bill passed the committee but was killed on the Senate floor.[11]

In 1994, McCain returned to Bath, Maine, for the commissioning of the second USS *John S. McCain*, a destroyer named for both his father and his grandfather. Returning to the shipbuilding city now as a full-grown adult and U.S. Senator, he found it was a far cry from his first visit when he was asked as a 17-year old if he drank liquor. This time, he was accompanied by Cindy and their oldest two children, Meghan and Jack. Former President George H.W. Bush was the speaker that day, and McCain stood proudly by as Cindy christened the new destroyer.

BOSNIA AND ROBERT J. DOLE

During the 1990s, McCain was honing his international experience and found himself in the middle of a political fight over deploying American troops to Bosnia, a an Eastern European country that had declared its independence in 1992 from the former nation of Yugoslavia. Yugoslavia, which had been created out of six existing nations under Communist rule, was breaking apart, and the breaking would not come easily. Serbian President Slobodan Milosevic sent armies to try to stop the secession. Meanwhile, Serbian rebels were fighting in Bosnia, and Christian Croats were fighting against Bosnian Muslims. The United Nations sent a peacekeeping force to the region, but there was no peace to keep.

NATO, the North American Treaty Organization, which included the United States, decided to get involved and to try to stop the war or at least to prevent civilians from being slaughtered.[12]

The United States sent planes but left most of the ground fighting to the European troops. By 1995, the United States had brokered a ceasefire in the region, and President Clinton agreed to send 20,000 troops. That decision was controversial, to say the least. Many Americans thought that the United States shouldn't be sending troops into an unstable situation. But Senate Majority Leader Bob Dole, a Kansas Republican who was severely wounded in World War II, believed that the United States had a moral obligation to send the troops to Bosnia and that he had the same moral obligation to support the president. So did McCain.

Congressional approval wasn't needed for the troop deployment, but McCain and Dole knew there would be some kind of vote on the Bosnian situation and that most members of the Senate were opposed. They teamed up to try to figure out how to get an affirmative vote backing the president.

Complicating matters was the fact that Dole was running for president in the election of 1996. Senator Phil Gramm, a Texas Republican, was running against Dole in the primaries. Gramm was also opposed to sending the troops to Bosnia. Gramm vowed to fight Dole on the resolution, knowing that he had the political high ground.

McCain and Dole went to work, trying to whip up support. The debate and vote took place in December 1995. Dole took to the floor to make an argument. McCain stayed in the back, listening. Dole made a few remarks about McCain as part of his speech about soldiers and sacrifice and the Vietnam War. Dole said he had argued then about not cutting off funding for the troops, including McCain, in Vietnam. His next sentence floored McCain.

"I was wearing a John McCain bracelet, proudly, a POW bracelet, and arguing with my Democratic colleagues not to cut off funding for the Vietnam War. I led the debate for seven weeks in an effort to derail those who would cut off funds while John McCain was in a little box over there," Dole said.

McCain never knew that Dole had worn his bracelet. In all their years together in the Senate, Dole had never told him about the bracelet, which was a popular symbol at the time, with many Americans wearing them as a reminder of various POWs, not just McCain. McCain choked up in the Senate chamber at that knowledge and celebrated with Dole later that night when their resolution to support the troops passed.[13]

Dole beat Gramm and several others in the Republican primaries in 1996 and went on to claim the Republican nomination to run against Clinton. There was some revived talk about making McCain the vice presidential nominee, but that job went to former Representative (and former professional football player) Jack Kemp. McCain was asked to formally nominate Dole at the Republican convention in San Diego.

Unpracticed as a public speaker in such a large forum, and with only a day's notice to prepare, McCain opted to tell the world what Dole had told him only months before—that Dole had worn McCain's POW bracelet. "Bob never told me he wore my bracelet. He never sought my thanks," McCain said, using the anecdote to illustrate that Dole was an unselfish, patriotic leader.[14]

"Although Bob Dole never asked me for recognition for his kindness to me, I have felt since learning of it, that this modest, good man deserved from me a heartfelt expression of gratitude. I wish to do so now," McCain said. "For myself, for my comrades who came home with me to the country we loved so dearly, and for the many thousands who did not: Thank you, Bob, thank you for the honor of your concern and support. We fought in different wars, but we keep the same faith. I shall always be grateful."[15]

Dole campaigned vigorously but was trailing Clinton, who was very popular at the time, for most of the election. In the last 96 hours, Dole decided to campaign nonstop. McCain went with him and watched as the vigorous 73-year-old Dole barnstormed around the country. In the end, he lost to Clinton, but he maintained his honor and wished Clinton well.

Two years later, McCain ran for re-election to the Senate and won in a cakewalk, defeating Democrat Ed Ranger, an environmental attorney who had no political experience. McCain took no "soft money" in his own race but still came up with $4.4 million for the campaign, saying he needed the money in case one of the special interests he had upset in Washington, such as the tobacco companies, came after him. Ranger charged he was collecting money to make a run for president. Ranger was right.[16]

NOTES

1. *Congressional Record*, April 20, 1994, p. S4512, http://thomas.loc.gov/cgi-in/query/F?r103:9:./temp/~r1036BmOjk:e61029.

2. Ibid.

3. Guy Gugliotta, "A Web-Wise Spin on the Pork Barrel," *Washington Post*, September 23, 1997, p. A15.

4. *Congressional Record*, October 21, 1998, p. S12822, http://thomas.loc.gov/cgi-bin/query/F?r105:26:./temp/~r105sqqlsC:e65562.

5. Associated Press, "Senate Rejects a Line-Item Veto," *New York Times*, February 28, 1992, http://query.nytimes.com/gst/fullpage.html?res=9E0CE6DE1530F93BA15751C0A964958260&scp=1&sq=mccain+pork+barrel&st=nyt.

6. David E. Rosenbaum, "Senate Approves Line-Item Veto for President," *New York Times*, March 28, 1996, http://query.nytimes.com/gst/fullpage.html?res=940DE2D61139F93BA15750C0A960958260&sec=&spon=&pagewanted=print.

7. John McCain with Mark Salter, *Worth the Fighting For* (New York: Random House, 2002), p. 358.

8. Michael Barone and Grant Ujifusa, *The Almanac of American Politics 1998* (Washington, DC: National Journal, 1997).

9. Elaine S. Povich, "No More Soft Money; Campaign Finance Overhaul Passes, Bush Says He'll Sign," *Newsday*, March 21, 2002, p. A5.

10. Ibid.

11. Paul Alexander, *Man of the People: The Life of John McCain* (Hoboken, NJ: Wiley, 2003), pp. 185–186.

12. Jason Austin, "U.S. Peacekeepers Complete Bosnia Mission," *National Guard Magazine*, December 2004, http://findarticles.com/p/articles/mi_qa3731/is_200412/ai_n9468157.

13. McCain, *Worth the Fighting For*, pp. 296–301.

14. Glenn Kessler, "All Dole: On Nomination Night, Wife, Daughter Tell Story," *Newsday*, August 15, 1996, pp. A4–A5.

15. "Speeches by Sen. McCain and Gov. Pataki Nominating Dole and Kemp," *New York Times*, August 15, 1996, http://query.nytimes.com/gst/fullpage.html?res=9D05E3D91331F936A2575BC0A960958260&sec=&spon=&pagewanted=2.

16. Dan Nowicki and Bill Muller, "McCain Profile: Chapter 9: McCain Becomes the 'Maverick,'" *Arizona Republic*, March 1, 2007, http://www.azcentral.com/news/election/mccain/articles/2007/03/01/20070301mccainbio-chapter9.html.

Chapter 16

"LIGHTNING IN A BOTTLE": RUNNING FOR PRESIDENT, 2000

With an easy Senate victory behind him, McCain called a meeting in January 1999 in his Senate office with some of his closest advisers. There was a new face among them. Mike Murphy, an experienced political consultant with an iconoclastic streak, was a perfect complement to McCain.

While McCain had begun thinking seriously about running for president as far back as 1995 (or maybe even before), the 1999 meeting was the first step toward actually running. John Weaver, McCain's political consultant and guru, had been informally recruiting staff for a potential run for a year.[1] It's one thing to look in the mirror and see a president looking back (as, it is said, almost every U.S. Senator does); it's another thing to actually run for president. And McCain knew that he would not have the backing of the Republican establishment because of his maverick stances. But there was something that appealed to him about being the outsider, underdog candidate. And Murphy had figured out a way to make it work. Murphy, a veteran of the 1992 election campaign when President George H. W. Bush lost to Bill Clinton and of several winning gubernatorial races, gave a 25-minute presentation. McCain was impressed. The campaign, which McCain himself termed a "long shot," was about to take off.[2]

The new "staff" (only a few were paid) knew something about their candidate that they found appealing and thought others would, too. His life's story was compelling.

"His honesty, his willingness to speak his mind and fight for what he believes in" drew press secretary Howard Opinsky back to Washington from Texas, where he had just moved. "He was the first politician that I felt more in sync with than most of the others I had worked for." Opinsky went back and read McCain's biography, particularly the part where, after the *Forrestal* fire, McCain volunteered to fly missions off the *Oriskany*.

"He had bravery and commitment that goes well beyond any I could hope to have," Opinsky said.[3]

At that point in the race, there were many candidates, all but one of whom—Bush—would drop out quickly. They were former Tennessee Governor Lamar Alexander, former undersecretary of education and Christian conservative Gary Bauer, conservative author Patrick Buchanan, former Secretary of Labor Elizabeth Dole (wife of Bob Dole), billionaire publisher Steve Forbes, Utah Senator Orrin Hatch, Ohio Representative John Kasich, conservative African American activist Alan Keyes, New Hampshire Senator Robert Smith, and former Vice President Dan Quayle.

McCain traveled around the country in preparation for the official announcement tour of his candidacy, which he hoped to make in April. But, internationally, events were taking place that would disrupt that timetable. Yugoslav leader Slobodan Milosevic ordered the mass killing of ethnic Albanians in the troubled Balkans region of Europe. President Bill Clinton wanted to send more American troops there. The decision was controversial, but the Congress, led by McCain and others, eventually agreed with Clinton.

McCain, his presidential aspirations already widely anticipated, took to the Senate floor to state his convictions.

"We must not permit the genocide that Milosevic has in mind for Kosovo to continue. We are at a critical hour," McCain said. And he warned that the operation would not be "casualty free."[4]

McCain's profile with the media, already high because of his role in campaign finance reform, was getting even higher with the military operation in the Balkans. He appeared often on television as a commentator on the war.

He was the subject of an A & E cable TV network biography about this life titled *John McCain: American Maverick*. The episode was widely viewed, and McCain's name identification—the number of people who knew who he was—immediately went up.

And he was about to publish an autobiographical book that would give him an opportunity to stage a book tour across the country that looked for all the world like a political campaign. *Faith of My Fathers: A Family Memoir*, written by McCain and Mark Salter, his long-time aide, became an instant best-seller. McCain signed autographs all across the country, from bookstores from The Mall of New Hampshire (a state that just happened to hold the first presidential primary the next year) to San Francisco (in California, a critical primary state).

Salter recalls that the hardest part of doing the book was getting McCain to agree to it in the first place. Although McCain was always conflicted about his relationship with his father and grandfather, they were nonetheless his role models—with all of their wisdom, skills, and flaws.

"He talked into a tape recorder," Salter said. "He's a natural. It was not a lot more complicated than writing it down." Salter's assessment understated his own writing abilities, but McCain is a natural storyteller. Salter recalled that when McCain came to the painful parts of his life, his normal loquaciousness would fade and he would become "monosyllabic," but he never stopped talking altogether.[5]

During the signing events, McCain was never monosyllabic. People lined up for hours to get a glimpse of him and to get his signature on a book, usually in bold script, written with a felt-tipped pen.

CAMPAIGN KICKOFF

McCain finally formally kicked off his campaign in September in New Hampshire, the state that holds the first presidential primary every four years. He had adopted a risky campaign strategy that called for him to skip the Iowa caucuses and concentrate on New Hampshire, instead. While the Iowa contest came before New Hampshire's and was the traditional place candidates went first to test their strength, the contest there was quirky. It required people to gather together in schools, churches, civic centers, or people's homes and to stand up publicly for their candidate rather than vote in secret in a booth. Mobilizing that many people took tremendous organization, something that McCain's primary rival, then Texas Governor George W. Bush, son of the former president, had plenty of and McCain very little. McCain also was opposed to government subsidies for ethanol (a fuel made out of corn that can be added to gasoline), which was produced abundantly in Iowa. That stance would not endear him to Iowans. McCain decided to skip Iowa altogether, except for one debate appearance.

Meanwhile, he was racking up appearances all over New Hampshire. Eventually, he would tally 114 town meetings. People in New Hampshire began to feel like they knew him.

But his campaign was critically short of money. Bush had been able to raise far more cash. So McCain's team—Weaver, Opinsky, Salter, Murphy, and others—hit on a strategy that would take advantage of McCain's ability to talk to news reporters. It was risky, but necessary. The team decided to let reporters ride on McCain's bus as he toured around the state. The bus was dubbed the "Straight Talk Express," after McCain's expression "Here's a little straight talk" that he liked to use in speeches.

Press secretary Howard Opinsky remembers that the technique evolved from allowing a reporter or two to ride with McCain in a car to having several reporters ride in a van. "We thought it up in a bar," Opinsky said. "It was going to be our biggest asset. The question was could we get reporters to come with us?"[6]

Todd Harris, the traveling press secretary, remembers that when the reporters did start to fill up the bus, McCain just naturally went to talk to them.

The bus was outfitted with a series of compartments, with the candidate and his aides usually occupying the front section, nearest the driver. There was a little kitchenette in the middle of the bus and a section with leather benches, a couple of armchairs, and writing tables for the press. The reporters were in the back. Early in the campaign, McCain got on the bus, "blew right past the staff and walked to the back of the bus, sat down with the media and started talking," Harris said.[7]

McCain sometimes jokingly referred to the press as "my base," but the technique worked. Members of the media, stunned by McCain's decision to just sit down and talk, every day, when most candidates would avoid them, played along. They asked McCain every question under the sun, from his favorite book (For Whom the Bell Tolls) and movie (Viva Zapata!) to his ideas about the newly emerging countries of Eastern Europe and how many nuclear weapons they had.

McCain never refused to answer a question. In return, the reporters sometimes gave him a pass on routine slipups, though not on major news. He once went on a tear about then-Attorney General Janet Reno's handling of the case of Elian Gonzalez, a little Cuban boy who got caught up in a dispute between family members that turned into a confrontation between the United States and Cuba, bashing her all over the place. Then he asked for, and was granted, a " do-over" for the traveling press, so that his words were toned down. While he was still critical, the language was softened.[8]

Once, when his wife Cindy was on the bus, the McCains retold the story of how they both had lied about their ages when they got married. Hopping off the bus, McCain launched into a campaign speech in which he promised voters to "always tell you the truth, no matter what."

Back on the "Straight Talk Express," he was asked about the contradiction. "That? That was a clerical error," he joked. Cindy McCain shook her head, and all within earshot were supposed to know the difference between his jokes and his campaign platforms. The reporters generally got it.[9]

While the "Straight Talk" technique succeeded in making friends out of the press and garnered lots of free publicity for McCain in the form of newspaper stories and broadcast pieces, it was not without peril. For example, one day, a reporter on the bus asked McCain what he would do if his then-teenage daughter, Meghan, became pregnant. McCain, who had always presented himself as being against abortion, replied that the decision would be "up to her." The anti-abortion conservatives in the Republican Party went crazy, and McCain was forced to reiterate his anti-abortion position and revise his answer about his daughter to say that it would be a family decision.

And then there was the confederate flag issue. South Carolina, one of the states that held its primary shortly after New Hampshire, had a controversial tradition of flying the Confederate flag—the "Stars and Bars" of Civil War vintage—over the state Capitol. Civil rights advocates were insulted by the flag; other people said it was part of the state's proud history.

Asked by CBS reporter Bob Schieffer in a *Face the Nation* television interview what the Confederate flag meant to him, McCain replied that the flag was "very offensive" to many Americans as a "symbol of racism and slavery" but that, as a descendant of Southerners, he understood its historical significance. His answer angered conservative voters in South Carolina who were critical to winning the primary there. Under pressure, he put out a statement "clarifying" his position. "As to how I view the flag, I understand both sides. Some view it as a symbol of slavery; others view it as a symbol of heritage. Personally, I see the battle flag as a symbol of heritage."[10]

As he pulled his statement from his breast pocket to read it to reporters, an embarrassed smile crossed his face, as if he knew he wasn't telling the truth with the clarification, but he did it anyway. Years later, he admitted that the "clarifying" statement had been a lie and that the lie was compounded by the fact that he had pledged to be truthful in his 2000 campaign.

> I had not pledged to tell the truth as much as circumstances allowed. I had not pledged to tell a lie only if it was apparent I really would have preferred not to. I had promised to tell the truth *no matter what.* When I broke it, I had not been just dishonest. I had been a coward, and I had severed my own interests from my country's. That was what made the lie unforgivable. All my heroes, fictional and real, would have been ashamed of me.[11]

The campaign went on, and New Hampshire paid little or no attention. The Confederate flag wasn't an issue in a state so far north that it shared a border with Canada.

McCain was barnstorming around New Hampshire on his bus, drawing larger and larger crowds. At one event, a woman came up to him wearing another of his POW bracelets, with the date of his shootdown, 10–26–67, saying that she had been waiting 30 years to meet him. Judy Tilton said her father, a retired lieutenant colonel in the National Guard, had given it to her when she was seven years old. McCain was touched. He usually didn't like to talk about his POW experience, but his personal story was a selling point in New Hampshire. His self-deprecating humor also worked. He consistently denied he was a hero, saying that it was not heroic to "intercept a Soviet-made surface-to-air missile with my own airplane."[12]

The independent voters of New Hampshire seemed to take McCain to their hearts. Polls began to show that he was leading. After having been at 6 percent in the polls a year earlier, he couldn't quite believe it.

On primary day, he thought about going to the movies, as he had every other election day (it had become a superstition) but decided to order a movie in his hotel room instead, figuring his going out would create a stir.

The early exit polls were encouraging. McCain and his aides said nothing so as not to jinx their luck. Then, as the day turned into a wintry night, the networks called the state for McCain. He was going to win the New Hampshire primary—and it was a rout. He bested Bush by 18 points.

"This has implications," McCain recalled saying.

"Gee, like you might be president. That might be one of them," McCain recalled Salter saying.[13]

A packed hotel ballroom rocked with McCain's victory party. Cindy McCain's hand flew to her mouth when CNN announced that her husband had won. "It really happened," she said, smiling and tearing up at the same time. Their two boys, Jimmy, 11, and Jack, 13, began dancing.

"My friends, a wonderful New Hampshire campaign has come to an end, but a great national crusade has just begun," McCain told his cheering supporters as he claimed victory. "As we embark on it together, I promise I will never forget you and the wisdom I learned here."[14]

It would be the highlight of his campaign.

SOUTH CAROLINA NASTINESS

It was after 1 A.M. when McCain, weary but pumped up, boarded his airplane for the flight to South Carolina, where he would begin campaigning for that state's primary. He landed at about 3 A.M. and drove the bus into an airport hangar where supporters, many of them college students, had been partying all night, waiting for him. He wowed the crowd again and barely had time for a nap before the day's campaigning began. But George Bush was not about to take the loss in New Hampshire lying down. He and his aides had said that the loss had made him a tougher fighter, and it had. Bush political mastermind Karl Rove immediately began using Bush's superior fundraising to run ads in the state and to batter McCain about the Confederate flag and campaign finance reform, which Bush said would hurt the Republican Party's ability to raise money.

The race was becoming increasingly ugly. Independent groups ran ads urging evangelicals not to vote for McCain because his adviser, New Hampshire Senator Warren Rudman, was Jewish and prejudiced against Christian voters. Old rumors about McCain being the "Manchurian candidate" resurfaced.

McCain got angry in his speeches and ran ads attacking Bush, as well. McCain accused Bush of distorting his positions. "Do we really want another politician in the White House America can't trust?" an ad said, a reference to President Bill Clinton, who had been impeached, but not convicted, for lying about a relationship with a White House intern.

But all the negativity was wearing on McCain. He eventually pulled all the negative ads because he didn't like the way the campaign was going. The most devastating blow of all was struck by unknown operatives. They circulated a rumor that McCain had fathered a black "love child" out of wedlock. For McCain, who had adopted daughter Bridget from an orphanage in Bangladesh, this was unconscionable. Flyers began to turn up on cars outside McCain rallies with the allegation. Staff members chased after those putting out the leaflets but couldn't catch them.[15]

McCain lost South Carolina to Bush by 11 points. The race would go on for another month, but the fatal blow had been struck.

McCain won the Arizona and Michigan primaries and then campaigned in New York and New England, where he had the support of many moderate Republicans, and in California, Ohio, and Washington State. Many of the state had primaries on "Super Tuesday," February 29, and McCain's campaign plane touched down in them all. He visited veterans' memorials in Rochester, New York, and city parks in San Diego, California.

But the campaign was running out of money and was having a hard time keeping up with Bush's well-financed campaign. McCain caused another stir among conservative evangelicals when he called evangelical preachers Pat Robertson and Jerry Falwell "agents of intolerance" and "forces of evil." He later apologized for the phrase, saying that because he often referred to the movie *Star Wars*, and it's "evil empire," in his campaign speeches, his comments may have been inadvertently juxtaposed with comments about the preachers.

As the results from Super Tuesday came in, McCain conceded that Bush had won the vast majority of the states. He then flew home to Arizona to figure out what to do.

He took one day at his rustic Sedona home to huddle with advisers. There was snow on the mountains and sprigs of green in the valleys mixed with the red rocks. The next day, he appeared before a stunning landscape, overlooking the Red Rock Mountains and the Verde Valley. He referred to the place as "my beautiful Arizona."

"I am no longer an active candidate for my party's nomination for president," McCain said. "I congratulate Governor Bush and wish him and his family well. He very well may become the next president of the United States. That is an honor accorded to very few, and it is such a great responsibility that he deserves the best wishes of every American. He certainly has mine."

McCain used the word "suspending" his campaign, but aides said it was over. "He ceased his campaign," said spokesman Howard Opinsky. "Today, he got out of the race."

Then, as a final gesture that would leave no doubt, Opinsky hurled his campaign-issued pager into the ravine. There would be no more calls from reporters about the "Straight Talk Express."[16]

Many months later, McCain took his busload of reporters for one last ride from Washington to the 2000 Republican convention, in Philadelphia. Seventy-five journalists signed up for the trip, forcing the campaign to stop twice along the way to swap out the reporters. Inevitably, he was asked, over and over, if he would run for president again. He wasn't sure.

The question, he said, was "could you replicate the kind of magic and excitement we were able to create? We caught lightning in a bottle and I don't know if we'd be able to create that again."[17]

It would be eight years before he would try to find out.

NOTES

1. Lanny Wiles, interview with author, Washington, DC, July 21, 2008.

2. John McCain with Mark Salter, *Worth the Fighting For* (New York: Random House, 2002), p. 365.

3. Howard Opinsky, interview with author, Washington, DC, July 28, 2008.

4. Greg McDonald, "Senate OKs Use of Force in Balkans," *Houston Chronicle*, March 23, 1999, http://www.chron.com/disp/story.mpl/world/218972.html.

5. Mark Salter, interview with author, Manchester, NH, September 7, 1999.

6. Howard Opinsky, interview with author, Washington, DC, July 28, 2008.

7. Todd Harris, interview with author, Washington, DC, July 25, 2008.

8. Ibid.

9. Elaine S. Povich, "Campaign Profile/A Combat Veteran," *Newsday*, March 3, 2000, p. A6.

10. McCain, *Worth the Fighting For*, p. 384.

11. Ibid., p. 386.

12. Dan Nowicki and Bill Muller, "McCain Profile: Chapter 10: The Maverick Runs," *Arizona Republic*, March 1, 2007 , http://www.azcentral.com/news/spe cials/mccain/articles/0301mccainbio-chapter10.html.

13. McCain, *Worth the Fighting For*, p. 368.

14. Ken Fireman and Elaine S. Povich, "Campaign 2000: McCain Reigns/Easily Beats Front-Runner Bush in New Hampshire," *Newsday*, February 2, 2000, p. A5.

15. Todd Harris, interview with author, Washington, DC, July 25, 2008.

16. Elaine S. Povich, "Campaign 2000/Out of the Running/McCain Ends on a Quiet Note—But Doesn't Endorse Bush," *Newsday*, March 10, 2000, p. A7.

17. CNN "All Politics," "McCain Rolls into Philadelphia Aboard Campaign Bus," July 29, 2000, http://archives.cnn.com/2000/ALLPOLITICS/stories/07/29/mccain.arrives/.

Chapter 17

A SENATOR WITH SWAY

McCain took a few days off after the end of this campaign, but only a few. He was hugely popular, even though he had lost, and was much in demand all over the nation to be a speaker for Republican candidates who were running for Congress.

Arriving back in the Senate, he was treated as a celebrity, though his first speech on his return, a speech about Kosovo and campaign finance reform, was made to an empty chamber but for the presence of Sen. Harry Reid, a Democrat from Nevada. His visit to the Republicans' weekly luncheon was akin to a rock star's arrival, however, complete with trailing camera crews, reporters, and gawking tourists.

He got a warm welcome from his fellow Republicans, but they continued to be skeptical about his campaign finance reform bill. Senator Larry Craig, R-Idaho, who was the third-highest ranking member of the GOP in the Senate, said McCain's bill "was not the reform agenda" of the Senate.[1]

McCain continued his campaigning for other Republicans around the country, but not Bush. Finally, in May 2000, McCain and Bush agreed to meet at an event in Pittsburgh, where McCain would endorse the Republican nominee. The meeting was tense, particularly between the staffs of the two candidates. Arrangements had been set up ahead of time. The first thing was that the two candidates would meet, alone, before their public appearance. Staff members waited in separate rooms. But, as the meeting dragged on well beyond the scheduled time, the staffs grew restless and finally migrated into the same room to wait together.

Bush and McCain appeared on the stage. Both were uncomfortable. McCain made a nice speech but never said explicitly that he endorsed

Bush. It took a reporter's question to finally get the words out of his mouth. "I endorse Governor Bush, I endorse Governor Bush, I endorse Governor Bush," McCain repeated. And it was over.[2]

In some ways, it was harder for McCain's staff to get over the loss than it was for McCain. McCain bucked up the staff by telling them that when you have endured the things that he had endured, particularly in Vietnam, losing an election wasn't really all that big a deal. "If you can move on from the worst, most unimaginable horror that can possibly exist and then forgive those that did it to you, losing a campaign seems pretty small by comparison," recalled Todd Harris.[3]

McCain then took a train trip with Bush through California and invited the Bushes to his cabin in Sedona, Arizona. It all seemed normal, if slightly strained, given the bitterness of their primary. But McCain was dealing with another issue, unknown to nearly everyone outside his family.

McCain had been diagnosed with melanoma, a deadly form of skin cancer. Fair-skinned and a sun-worshipper in his youth, he was a prime candidate for skin cancer. He had had some earlier benign lesions removed without incident, but this was something much more serious.

After the weekend with Bush, McCain went to the Mayo Clinic in Minnesota to have the lesions removed. The surgery was successful, but it left him with an ugly scar that ran down the left side of his face. He recovered fully, however, and joked about his latest brush with death, saying repeatedly, then and later throughout his career, that he has "more scars than Frankenstein."

It certainly was just the latest of many near-death experiences for him, beginning with the ditching of planes into the ocean, even before Vietnam, through the USS *Forrestal* fire, and the entire POW experience. It was enough to make him spiritual.

"I do have this kind of belief that I may be the luckiest person I have ever heard of in my life, when you look at the number of occasions when I survived when it was not likely," he said years after all of the experiences were behind him.[4]

McCain mostly sat out the rest of the 2000 presidential election, though he did make many appearances for House candidates. When the 2000 presidential contest was so close that ballots in Florida were counted and recounted and the Supreme Court finally stepped in to the fray to say that the recounts were to end, clearing the way for George W. Bush to finally be declared the winner weeks later over Al Gore, McCain was quiet. He was still planning to do good work in the Senate, no matter who was president, but he would now have to contend with Bush again.

CAMPAIGN FINANCE—FINALLY

Despite his presidential loss, McCain found he had increased clout in the Senate. His popularity and his campaign work on behalf of Republicans had made him into a power to be contended with. That power would soon put him at odds with Bush once again.

The Senate was divided 50–50 at the start of 2001, with Republicans in charge by virtue of Vice President Richard Cheney's tie-breaking dual role as President of the Senate. But, because of the closely divided body, every vote was crucial to getting legislation passed, and deals had to be struck with members of the opposite party. On May 24, 2001, Senator James Jeffords, a Vermont Republican, left his party and became an Independent, caucusing with the Democrats. Democrats were then in control, but also by an eyelash.

Also thrown into the mix was the fact that the Senate needed 60 votes on controversial legislation—the number necessary to break a filibuster (a talk-a-thon) on any bill. Campaign finance reform, McCain's premier issue, was such a bill, so he needed 60 votes. The closest he had come to that total was 59 votes the year before, while he was running.

But, in January 2001, Senator Thad Cochran, a Mississippi Republican, decided to break the logjam. He declared that he would now support the McCain-Feingold bill, at least long enough to break the filibuster and bring the issue to a vote.

That was all the ammunition McCain and Feingold needed. With the new Democratic majority and Cochran's support, campaign finance reform crashed through the Senate on a 59–41 vote. The bill banned "soft money," the unregulated and unlimited money from corporate and union political action committees. It also limited advertising 60 days before an election.

McCain was vindicated, at last. In his last comments before the vote, McCain said, "I asked at the start of this debate for my colleagues to take a risk for America. In a few moments, I believe we will do just that. I will go to my grave deeply grateful for the honor of being a part of it." [5]

The House was also split on the issue, and Republican leaders were trying to prevent the campaign finance bill from coming to the floor. It took a rare move by supporters—something called a "discharge petition"—to wrest the bill out of committee and bring it to the floor over the objections of the GOP leadership. It passed overwhelmingly once it got to the floor. But compromises had to be made, and the bill looked different from the Senate's. It would take almost another year for the differences to be ironed out and for the bill to finally pass. President Bush signed it, quietly, with no fanfare. McCain was not invited to the White House for the signing ceremony.

MR. CLOUT

Aside from campaign finance reform, McCain found that he had much maneuvering room in the Senate, more than he had ever had before. Because he was not marching in lockstep with the Republicans, they had to court him to get his vote. Because he had taken some stands with Democrats, he was valuable to them, as well. And he had learned some things on the campaign trail. All of those town meetings had made him sensitive to domestic issues that he hadn't given much time to in his previous years in the Senate. He had mostly concentrated on foreign policy, military issues, and an occasional pork-barrel fight. But now, he was branching out.

"I worked on various reform issues," McCain said. "But also one of the biggest issues that I didn't think about before the primary was climate change.

"I worked with [Senator Joseph] Lieberman [a Connecticut Democrat turned Independent] and others on cap and trade," he said, referring to legislation aimed at curbing atmospheric emissions from manufacturing plants that many Republicans were opposed to.[6]

Throughout 2001, McCain continued to be a thorn in Bush's side. He teamed up with Democratic Senators Edward Kennedy of Massachusetts and John Edwards of North Carolina on a HMO "patients' bill of rights." He criticized Bush for blocking an international treaty on climate control, and he again teamed up with Lieberman on a bill that called for more regulation of firearms sold at gun shows.

He refused to pile on with the criticism of many in his party when Jeffords bolted, leading to speculation that he might be the next to cross the line over to the Democrats. Fueling that speculation was a longstanding invitation he had issued months earlier to Democratic Majority Leader Tom Daschle and his wife to visit the McCains at their Arizona cabin. He was quick to deny that the visit was anything but a social occasion and added that, no, he wasn't changing parties.

And McCain hit Bush on one of his most important issues, becoming only one of two Republicans to vote against Bush's $1.35 trillion tax-cut package, saying the cuts benefited the wealthy but not ordinary Americans.[7]

He supported scientific research using embryonic stem cells that might lead to breakthroughs against disease; Bush opposed it on grounds that it might destroy otherwise healthy embryos.

He was the only Republican to vote against a 2001 water projects bill.

And he teamed with Democrat John Kerry on a bill to require cars to get higher miles per gallon of gasoline, something favored by environmentalists.[8]

On September 11, 2001, McCain was in his office when the terrorists' planes hit the World Trade Center's twin towers that morning and another plane dived into the Pentagon just across the Potomac River from the Capitol. A fourth plane, possibly headed for the Capitol itself, crashed in rural Pennsylvania, its suicide bombers having been overpowered by determined passengers.

He spoke out strongly against the attacks and began working for a bipartisan commission to investigate. He supported Bush in his decision to attack Afghanistan to root out Al Qaeda, the terrorist organization responsible for the attacks on U.S. soil. And he put the commission idea into legislation, which was approved. The commission investigated every aspect of the attacks, with the idea that more knowledge might go a long way toward preventing a similar attack on U.S. soil.

McCain also supported President Bush's decision to invade Iraq to stop Iraqi leader Saddam Hussein from building weapons of mass destruction and from harboring terrorists. While McCain would later come to question the conduct of the Iraqi war, he voted for it in the beginning.

Once again, McCain was sought after as a commentator on the wars and terrorism. And he again played to the media, appearing on countless television shows, in countless newspapers and websites.

And he was also honing his skills in the Senate, learning to be a player, not just an iconoclast. He returned with new interest in the Senate and took on more issues, and his popularity with Democrats and Independents gave him more clout. And he had learned how to play the game even better than before.

TRIANGULATION

McCain became the essential ingredient for compromise in the closely divided Senate. He had plenty of political capital, and he intended to use it.

He worked for President Bush's re-election in 2004, squelching rumors that he would bolt the Republican Party and run as an independent. But, once the election was over, he continued to strike out on his own path.

He pushed the Bush administration to sign laws banning the use of torture on military detainees, particularly those prisoners from the Iraq

War held at the U.S. military base in Guantanamo, Cuba. His stature as a former POW gave him additional power—it was hard to argue for torture against someone who had been tortured and survived.

In 2005, Senate Majority leader Bill Frist, a Tennessee Republican, was embroiled in a standoff with Senate Democrats over some judges that President Bush wanted to appoint to federal courts. The issue of judicial appointments had been simmering for years and had escalated into threats about shutting down the Senate or rewriting Senate rules governing debates—redoing the filibuster rule, for example, which had stood for decades.

McCain publicly supported Frist but privately began negotiations to put together a group of Democrats and Republican who could find a compromise. Eventually known as the "Gang of 14," the group came up with a deal to confirm some of the judges and stop Frist from rewriting the rules. McCain was again seen as a bipartisan player. And Frist's star fell. Frist had thought about running for president, but those hopes seemed doomed after the McCain move.[9]

Questions were beginning to mount about whether McCain would run for president again. In *Worth the Fighting For*, written shortly after the 2000 election, he wrote: "I did not get to be President of the United States. And I doubt I shall have reason or opportunity to try again. I could leave [Congress] now satisfied that I have accomplished enough things that I believe are useful to the country to compensate for the disappointment of my mistakes."[10]

But that book was written before the country had time to process the September 11, 2001, attacks, the Afghanistan War, and, most especially, the Iraq War, which became a long-term conflict.

More and more questions were beginning to be raised about whether McCain might take the plunge again—and whether, at age 71, he would be willing and ready to try again.

NOTES

1. Elaine S. Povich, "McCain Returns to Senate," *Newsday*, March 22, 2000, p. A19.

2. Elaine S. Povich, "'Taking His Medicine,' McCain Endorses Bush," *Newsday*, May 10, 2000, p. A10.

3. Todd Harris, interview with author, Washington, DC, July 25, 2008.

4. John McCain, interview with author, Washington, DC, July 25, 2008.

5. Allison Mitchell, "Campaign Finance Bill Passes in Senate, 59–41; House Foes Vow a Fight," *New York Times*, April 3, 2001, p. A1.

6. John McCain, interview with author, Washington, DC, July 25, 2008.

7. Dan Nowick and Bill Muller, "McCain Profile: Chapter 11: 'The Maverick' and President Bush," *Arizona Republic*, March 1, 2007.

8. Michael Barone, *The Almanac of American Politics 2004* (Washington, DC: National Journal, 2003).

9. David D. Kirkpatrick, "After 2000, McCain Learned to Work Levers of Power," *New York Times*, July 21, 2008, http://www.nytimes.com/2008/07/21/us/politics/21mccain.html?scp=1&sq=%22AFter%202000,%20McCain%22&st=cse.

10. John McCain with Mark Salter, *Worth the Fighting For* (New York: Random House, 2002), pp. 393–394.

Chapter 18

RUNNING AGAIN: CAMPAIGN 2008

For a few years, at least, running for president again seemed unlikely, even in McCain's mind. But, by mid-2006, it was clear he was running again. What had changed? Nothing. And everything.

"The commitment to service and the challenges the country faced," McCain said in describing his motives to run again.

The commitment to service was the same as in 2000. But the challenges were completely different.

"In 2000, we were still enjoying the benefits of the end of the Cold War," he said, in between campaign stops in Washington, DC, and Aspen, Colorado. "Here we are in 2008, in two wars against radical Islamic extremism. And I've still got the same motivation I had in 2000: to inspire a generation of young Americans to serve a cause greater than their self-interest."[1]

But this time, he would not be the happy warrior, the underdog candidate. This time, big things were expected of him. He began the campaign with high numbers in the political polls. But he had a problem. The campaign of 2000—the insurgent, outsider's campaign—had alienated many members of the Republican Party, particularly conservatives and evangelicals, who regarded his put-downs and dismissals of their beliefs as heresy. People tended to romanticize the 2000 McCain campaign, but as McCain repeatedly pointed out, he lost.

This time, it might be different. But, first, he had to figure out a way to get back into good graces with constituencies important to the Republican Party.

He started courting them. He famously returned to Liberty University, home of the Reverend Jerry Falwell, to give a commencement address in May 2006. Falwell was one of those he had denounced as "evil" and an "agent of intolerance" during the 2000 campaign. What was this about, his incredulous supporters and the media wanted to know?

Jon Stewart of Comedy Central's *The Daily Show* wondered if the Straight Talk Express had "been rerouted through Bull [expletive] Town. Are you freaking out on us?" Stewart asked McCain. At least McCain's response was honest.

"Just a little," McCain responded. [2]

It was not a "freak out" but rather a calculated -tightrope-walking act. McCain had to balance his appeal to Democrats and independents (he had been frequently mentioned as a possible vice presidential candidate in 2004, but, that time, on the *Democratic* ticket with fellow Vietnam veteran Senator John Kerry of Massachusetts; he turned it down) with the need to win the *Republican* primary.

He delivered the same speech that he gave at Liberty University at the liberal New School, a college in New York headed by his former Senate colleague and fellow Vietnam veteran Bob Kerrey of Nebraska. At the New School, students turned their back on him and booed, another example of how difficult it would be for him to find middle ground.

McCain had defeated his opponent in his 2004 Senate re-election, the little-known Democratic schoolteacher Stuart Starky, with 77 percent of the vote, while collecting more than $2 million in campaign contributions—seed money for the presidential race.

His balancing act also included squaring his opposition to President Bush's conduct of the war in Iraq with support for the war itself. Within months of the invasion of Iraq, which he supported, McCain had said that there were not enough troops on the ground to do the job. As the war began to go badly in 2006, he began calling for more troops. Finally, he supported the 2007 increase in troops and claimed that the strategy was working. But much of the nation was still opposed to the war and wanted U.S. troops home quickly. Democrats jumped on that bandwagon and used it to win elections in 2006. It was their major theme in the 2008 presidential election.

But McCain held firm. "I would much rather lose a campaign than a war," he said.[3]

In Washington, McCain continued to support Bush in some things, but not others. He voted to extend the Bush tax cuts, which he had initially opposed. But he teamed with liberal Senator Edward Kennedy, a Massachusetts Democrat, on legislation to address the growing issue of illegal immigration. McCain was very familiar with immigration, since he came from a border state, The Kennedy-McCain bill would have put illegal immigrants on a path to legality; illegal immigrants could have gotten two three-year visas and then gone to the "back of the line" of legal immigrants awaiting citizenship.[4] But conservatives balked, and even when Kennedy and McCain added stronger enforcement against illegal immigration on the borders, the bill failed to pass.

McCain returned to New Hampshire, the site of his greatest victory in 2000, to start the 2008 campaign. It was a raw day in April 2007 when he addressed the people he always called "my friends."

"My friends, you can't sell me on hopelessness. You can't convince me our problems are insurmountable. Our challenges are an opportunity to write another chapter of American greatness," he said.[5]

McCain started out as the Republican frontrunner, buoyed by polls and his nearly universal name recognition from the last presidential race. But his tightrope act and his support of the immigration bill and an increasingly unpopular war made the race difficult. Former New York Mayor Rudolph Giuliani, viewed as a hero for his actions after the September 11, 2001, attacks devastated his city, surged ahead. And conservatives, not satisfied with McCain's attempt to mollify them, were looking for an alternative candidate. Some other possibilities started to emerge, including former Arkansas Governor Mike Huckabee, former Massachusetts Governor Mitt Romney, Senator Sam Brownback of Kansas, and Representative Ron Paul of Texas, who was something of a gadfly. Huckabee briefly became the darling of conservatives, who poured money into his shoestring campaign. Senator Fred Thompson jumped in, got a lot of press and high poll numbers, but then got out. A couple of other minor candidates did also, mostly because the conservative wing of the party was still looking for options other than McCain.

Though he had signed up senior Republican and Bush campaign strategists and fundraisers to work for him this time around, fundraising started to fall off. The McCain 2008 campaign, unlike the ragtag operation of 2000 that depended on "free media" reporters, was based on the expectation that millions in funds would come in. It hired the best ad makers and the best strategists and put together a gold-plated operation that was designed to scare off any other challengers and have McCain sweep into the nomination. But the money wasn't there. And the challengers were.

In the first three months of 2007, McCain took in $13 million, whereas Romney took in $23 million ($2.35 million of it from Romney's own fortune) and Giuliani, $15 million.[6] Democratic candidates were taking in even more.

The next quarter, fundraising was even worse, and expensive staff, travel, and other spending had taken McCain's war chest down to only $2 million—a pittance in campaign terms. McCain had to do something, and he did, shaking the campaign to its core. He fired two top aides, including John Weaver, who had been with him since the very beginnings of the 2000 race and whom he once viewed almost as a surrogate son, calling the perpetually serious Weaver "Sunny," tongue-in-cheek. The shakeup left the campaign reeling.[7] But McCain, in a way, was liberated. With polls showing him once again behind, he could play the role he loved the best—scrappy underdog.

He denied rumors that he would be dropping out soon, using his favorite black humor phrase from China's Communist dictator Mao Zedong: "Things always look darkest before they turn completely black." But he kept on running. He told supporters that he wasn't very good at fundraising but that he would be a good president.

The staff shakeup and the new barebones campaign brought out the old McCain.

And he started spending a lot of time in New Hampshire, Iowa, and South Carolina, the first three primary contests of the 2008 race—and especially campaigned in New Hampshire.

At a town hall meeting (McCain's favorite venue) in Concord, New Hampshire., a teenager rose to ask McCain about his age and whether he was worried about developing Alzheimer's disease or dying in office. McCain's age was a touchy issue in the campaign, since he was the oldest of all the candidates.

As the audience tittered at the brashness of the question, McCain noted that he was very vigorous and energetic and had outcampaigned everyone he'd ever run against, and he cited his 95-year-old mother, Roberta, in the audience, as evidence of his good genes. Then he added: "Thanks for the question, you little jerk. You're drafted."[8]

The old McCain was back.

He campaigned even more vigorously, helped by the presence of his family, especially Cindy and his daughter Meghan, who started a campaign blog in an effort to woo younger voters. His old POW buddies came onto the campaign trail with him, and they further shored him up.

Campaigning in Florida, McCain whipped off another one-liner that showed his old spark. Senator Hillary Clinton of New York was campaigning for the Democratic presidential nomination and had sponsored a little bill to give $1 million to a museum commemorating the 1969 Woodstock music and arts festival—a four-day event that became a symbol for the hippie counterculture of the 1960s. McCain and many Republicans looked on the event with disdain.

"Now, my friends, I wasn't there," McCain said at a Republican debate in Florida. "I'm sure it was a cultural and pharmaceutical event. I was tied up at the time."

The audience, and even some of his Republican rivals, laughed and applauded McCain's line about being held in a Vietnamese prison while the hippies were partying at home.[9]

McCain was gaining on his rivals, and the contours of the race were beginning to favor him, as well. Brownback dropped out and endorsed McCain, giving him a little bit of an "in" with conservatives. Huckabee had captured most of the conservative mantle, however, and he roared past Romney to win the Iowa caucuses on January 23, 2008. McCain came in third but was very much in the race.

Romney then staked his campaign on New Hampshire, just to the north of his native Massachusetts. But New Hampshire was McCain territory.

McCain won the New Hampshire primary just as he had eight years earlier. It was just as sweet. "Mac is back!" chanted the celebrants at his victory party, held in the same hotel where he had celebrated his earlier victory.

"My friends, you know, I'm past the age when I can claim the noun 'kid,' no matter what adjective precedes it," a jubilant McCain said, alluding to President Bill Clinton's naming himself the "comeback kid" after the New Hampshire primary back in 1992.

"But tonight, we sure showed 'em what a comeback looks like. When the pundits declared us finished, I told them, 'I'm going to New Hampshire, where the voters don't let you make their decision for them.'"[10]

Romney won the Michigan primary, but that was just a bump in the road for McCain. He went on to South Carolina, the scene of his most devastating loss eight years earlier. This time, there would be no whisper campaign, no leaflets claiming he had an "illegitimate black daughter." Bridget, by this time 15 and old enough to Google herself and learn about the hatred, was devastated, but her parents consoled her, and they moved on as a family.

The victory in South Carolina was doubly sweet because he had triumphed over hate.

"It took us a while, but what's eight years among friends?" McCain said in his victory speech, continuing his ability to not hold (much of) a grudge.[11]

McCain went on to win the Florida primary and forced Giuliani, who had made a last stand there, out of the race. Then, on February 5, McCain won a majority of the "Super Tuesday" delegates, something else that had eluded him in 2000, and was well on his way to the nomination. Romney dropped out. McCain continued to win primaries and amassed enough Republican delegates by March to be the nominee of his party.

"The contest begins tonight," McCain said, claiming the nomination. "We will fight every minute of every day to make certain we have a government that is as capable, wise, brave and decent as the great people we serve. That's our responsibility, and I won't let you down."

NOTES

1. John McCain, interview with author, Washington, DC, July 25, 2008.

2. Dan Nowicki and Bill Muller, "McCain Profile: Chapter 12: The 'Maverick' Goes Establishment," *Arizona Republic*, March 1, 2007, http://www.azcentral. com/news/election/mccain/articles/2007/03/01/20070301mccainbio-chapter12. html.

3. Jamie Crawford, "Iraq Won't Change McCain," CNN Political Ticker, July 28, 2007, http://politicalticker.blogs.cnn.com/2007/07/28/iraq-wont-change-mccain/.

4. Michael Barone and Richard E. Cohen, *The Almanac of American Politics 2008* (Washington, DC: National Journal, 2007).

5. Dan Nowicki, "McCain Profile: Chapter 13: A Bumpy Start to the Campaign," *Arizona Republic*, July 15, 2008, http://www.azcentral.com/news/election/mccain/articles/2008/07/15/20080715mccainbio-chapter13.html.

6. Ibid.

7. Adam Nagourney and David D. Kirkpatrick, "McCain Campaign Drops Top Aides; New Doubts Rise," *New York Times*, July 11, 2007, http://www.ny times.com/2007/07/11/us/politics/11mccain.html?sq=mccain%20campaign&st=nyt&scp=1&pagewanted=print.

8. YouTube, "Raw Video: You Little Jerk, McCain Laughs," http://www.you tube.com/watch?v=F2zx3-0zOPs.

9. Dan Balz and Michael D. Shear, "Attacks Sharpen among Party's Principal Rivals," *Washington Post*, October 22, 2007, p. A1.

10. Remarks by John McCain on New Hampshire Primary Victory, January 8, 2008, John McCain for President Web site, http://www.johnmccain.com.

11. John McCain for President Web site, featured videos, South Carolina victory speech, January 19, 2008, www.johnmccain.com.

Chapter 19

MR. PRESIDENT?

Having sewn up the Republican nomination, McCain turned his attention to running against the Democrats. In the election of 2008, the Democrats had a long, drawn-out primary season, with senators Barack Obama of Illinois and Hillary Rodham Clinton of New York competing head to head for the right to carry the Democratic banner into the election against McCain. Senator John Edwards, a North Carolina Democrat, was in the race for a while but dropped out, leaving the two major candidates.

McCain had history with both Clinton and Obama. Surprisingly, he got along with Clinton, though they came from different parties. Clinton was more liberal, McCain more conservative. But they shared a love of public service and a commitment to gaining a generous amount of knowledge on important issues.

As fellow senators, they had traveled abroad often, visiting Iraq, the Baltic states of Eastern Europe, and several other farflung places. On their long flights together they began a friendship that was cemented in 2004 on a trip to Estonia during which they engaged in a legendary vodka-drinking contest, mimicking local custom. Clinton suggested the competition; McCain readily agreed. While memories apparently were foggy about who drank how much, McCain afterward proclaimed Clinton "one of the guys."[1]

Their apparent friendship led to some friendly speculation about them running together, an idea that was quickly squelched by both sides. Yet each respected the other.

Obama's relationship to McCain was another story. They initially appeared to get along after Obama first came to the Senate in 2005 and spoke briefly about an ethics reform bill that McCain was working on. McCain apparently got the impression that Obama was willing to work on a bipartisan compromise on the bill, which was to address lobbying reforms. But, in a February 2 "Dear John" letter to McCain, Obama said he was backing the Democratic Party's bill, instead. McCain was incensed and responded with an acidly worded "Dear Sen. Obama" letter "apologizing" for "assuming that your private assurances to me . . . were sincere." He also was upset that Obama released his letter to the media before McCain saw it.

McCain foreshadowed the presidential race to come when he noted tartly in his letter that he understood "how important the opportunity to lead your party's effort to exploit this issue must seem to a freshman Senator, and I hold no hard feelings over your earlier disingenuousness. Again, I have been around long enough to appreciate that in politics the public interest isn't always a priority for every one of us. Good luck to you, Senator."[2]

The two "made up" in a posed session before cameras, pointedly shaking hands and hugging each other, but they were not ever close.

After Obama made history by becoming the first African American to be nominated for president by a major party when he bested Clinton in the primaries, the 2008 race was joined. McCain apparently felt Obama continued to be a bit too full of himself. When Obama publicly toured Europe, to fawning receptions from gigantic crowds, McCain came out with a political ad poking fun at him as if he were Moses parting the Red Sea and another ad implying he was a worldwide celebrity. Both ads, however, questioned Obama's credentials to lead the nation.

McCain began his 2008 general election campaign by reprising his life with a "biography" tour. He visited Meridian, Mississippi, home to his ancestors and where he had served at a naval air station. He returned to Episcopal High School in Alexandria, Virginia, to the Naval Academy in Annapolis, Maryland, to Jacksonville, Florida, where he was stationed before Vietnam, and spoke of how his experiences in these places had shaped his life. And he gave a speech at the Yavapai County Courthouse in Prescott, Arizona, where he always ended his Senate campaigns. It was also the site where former Arizona Senator Barry Goldwater, a Republican, had declared his candidacy for the presidency. McCain pointed to that service and that of former Arizona Senator Mo Udall, a Democrat, in wrapping up the story of his life for the campaign. McCain noted of both Goldwater and Udall that, while far apart ideologically, "neither man ever had any doubt that the other acted at all times out of devotion to Arizona and the United States."[3]

Many people knew of McCain's history, but there were enough potential voters that did not know about him that he felt he could re-introduce himself to the nation yet again.

He challenged Obama by proposing a series of "town hall"-style meetings, where member of the audience would be allowed to pose unscripted questions. McCain excelled at this kind of format. But Obama balked. Obama was much better speaking to large crowds and rallying support that way.

The campaigns did agree to have the candidates meet in three debates.

McCain campaigned around the country, tackling the big issues of the day: health care, Social Security, climate change, the high price of oil, the Iraq war, and the economy. Economics was not McCain's strength, but he recognized that when the country is hurting, Americans want their presidential candidates to talk about the economy and to propose ways of handling the economy. McCain called for lowering taxes and cutting spending.

He began the general campaign running behind, partially because of the bad economic times. Voters were thinking that it might be time for a Democratic president after eight years of George Bush, a Republican. They did not seem predisposed to go with another Republican, even if that Republican (McCain) had pointed differences with Bush.

But, as spring turned into summer, McCain was gaining. By the force of his personality, his energy and his patriotism, he was turning an election that should have been a cakewalk for Democrats into a close contest, helped by the fact that some American voters were uneasy about Obama's relatively slight experience.

McCain had started out the campaign on a high note, focusing on his experience and biography, as the two Democratic candidates sparred. But, once the nominee was chosen, he went more negative—maintaining that Obama, with his polished speaking style and handsome features, had "celebrity" but not substance. As the two went into their respective conventions in late summer, McCain was behind Obama but closing.

At the Republican convention in St. Paul, Minnesota, he shocked the party, the press, and the nation by choosing little-known Alaska Governor Sarah Palin as his vice presidential running mate. After evaluating several of his Republican rivals for the nomination as possible vice presidents and teasing the country and his party by considering Democrat-turned-Independent Joseph Lieberman as a possibility, he decided to go with Palin, instead.

Palin thus became the first woman to run for vice president on the Republican ticket, matching what Geraldine Ferraro had done in 1984 for the Democrats. Palin was only two years into her term as governor, leading to charges that she was too inexperienced to be "a heartbeat away" from the presidency, serving with the man who would be the oldest president ever in his first term. But McCain stood by his nominee, showing stubborn admiration. He praised her as a reformer and a "maverick" just like himself.

The two hit the campaign trail after a rousing convention in which McCain pledged to be agents of change, despite the fact that his party, the Republicans, had controlled the White House for eight years. He said he was a politician who is not afraid to challenge the establishment, whether that establishment is of his party or another party. And he evoked his personal history as a way to give voters a measure of himself.

"I'm not running for president because I think I'm blessed with such personal greatness that history has anointed me to save our country in its hour of need," he said in his speech accepting the nomination. "My country saved me. My country saved me, and I cannot forget it. And I will fight for her for as long as I draw breath, so help me God."

"I fell in love with my country when I was a prisoner in someone else's," he added. "I loved it not just for the many comforts of life here. I loved it for its decency; for its faith in the wisdom, justice and goodness of its people. I loved it because it was not just a place, but an idea, a cause worth fighting for. I was never the same again. I wasn't my own man anymore. I was my country's."[4]

McCain left the convention upbeat and hit the campaign trail hard. At times, he seemed to be laid back about the campaign, but anyone who spent time around him knew that he wasn't planning on losing. But if he did, he would probably exercise another one of those more than nine lives he seems to have and keep on going.

"I can tell you right now, he can't stand losing," said top aide and co-author Mark Salter. "And sometimes when he's losing, it's not all romantic and glorious. He gets pretty tough. . . . He's as resilient a human being as I've ever encountered. There are no permanent defeats for him."[5]

His life illustrated the lack of "permanent" defeats every day that he lived it.

In a speech in 2000, he allowed himself to reflect on his life.

"My grandfather was an aviator; my father a submariner," he said. "They gave their lives to their country. In Tokyo Harbor, on the day the Japanese surrendered [after World War II], they were re-united for the last time. My grandfather would die a few days later. His last words to my father were 'it's an honor to die for your country and your principles.' I have been an imperfect servant of my country for over forty years, and my many mistakes rightly humble me. But I am their son . . . and they taught me to love my country, and that has made all the difference, my friends, all the difference in the world."[6]

NOTES

1. Anne E. Kornblut, "2008 May Test Clinton's Bond with McCain," *New York Times*, July 29, 2006, http://www.nytimes.com/2006/07/29/washington/29rivals. html?pagewanted = print.

2. Sen. Obama and Sen. McCain Exchange Letters on Ethics Reform," February 6, 2006, http://obama.senate.gov/letter/060206-sen_obama_and_sen_mccain_exchange_letters_on_ethics_reform/.

3. John McCain for President Web site, "Service to America: John McCain's remarks in Prescott, Arizona," April 5, 2008, http://www.johnmccain.com/Informing/News/Speeches/bb119770-c331–4e10-bc11–5e45a6c5b20c.htm.

4. John McCain, speech to the Republican National Convention, September 4, 2008, St. Paul, MN. http://www.johnmccain.com/Informing/News/Speeches/ef046a10-706a-4dd5-bd01-b93b36b054bc.htm.

5. Robert G. Kaiser, "The Curious Mind of John McCain: Ambition and Emotion Color the Complex Intellect of the Candidate," *Washington Post*, August 1, 2008, p. A1/.

6. *The Newshour with Jim Lehrer*, PBS television, August 1, 2000, transcript. http://www.pbs.org/newshour/election2000/gopconvention/john_mccain.html.

EPILOGUE

The crowd in the Ballroom of the Arizona Biltmore Resort on November 4, 2008, was subdued. This was not to be the victory party they had hoped for even in the face of polling data that showed their candidate trailing in the final weeks of the presidential campaign.

The major television networks had just called the election for Barack Obama. Now it was McCain's turn to speak.

After telephoning Obama in Chicago to congratulate him and offer any help he needed, McCain and Cindy, wearing a bright gold suit but with her eyes downcast, mounted the stage.

In contrast to a campaign that in the final month had spewed attacks and put-downs toward his rival, McCain's speech was gracious, heartfelt, and recognized the historic victory of his opponent, the first African American President of the United States.

The speech evoked McCain's history of service to the nation and harkened back to his roots—where his campaigns all started—and his commitment to America. Gone were the attacks, gone were the jibes; all that remained was McCain's core.

"Today, I was a candidate for the highest office in the country I love so much. And tonight, I remain her servant. That is blessing enough for anyone, and I thank the people of Arizona for it," he said.[1]

McCain talked of the "beautiful Arizona evening" on which his speech was made, recalling the "my beautiful Arizona" of his concession speech eight years earlier. He spoke of how Obama had inspired a "special pride" in African Americans and of his long held belief that "America offers opportunities to all who have the industry and will to seize it." That brought back memories of his friendship with Mexican American Frank Gamboa at the Naval Academy, not to mention his adoption of a dark-skinned Bangladeshi baby.

McCain wove in a tale of his favorite president, Theodore Roosevelt, saying that a century earlier "TR" had invited Booker T. Washington, the black educator and leader of Tuskegee University who rose from slavery to be one of the most prominent African Americans in the nation at that time, to the White House. This, McCain said, "was taken as an outrage in many quarters."

"America today is a world away from the cruel and frightful bigotry of that time," McCain said. "There is no better evidence of this than the election of an African-American to the presidency of the United States."[2]

Not included in the speech, but evident symbolism nonetheless, was the fact that McCain's headquarters for the night at the Biltmore was the resort's 1,157-square-foot Goldwater presidential suite, named for Senator Barry Goldwater, whom McCain succeeded in the Senate and who in 1964 also ran unsuccessfully for president. Maybe old Mo Udall was right, McCain may have been thinking, Arizona is still the state where mothers don't tell their children that they can grow up to be president.

The last few weeks of the campaign had been a struggle for McCain. He tried repeatedly to "change the conversation," to redirect the focus of the campaign to topics more favorable to him. But circumstances and missteps conspired against him.

In mid-September, a severe financial crisis hit the country. The stock market dropped drastically, major banks collapsed, and a giant insurance company sought help from the federal government. McCain's first response, a line he had delivered many times in his stump speech, was to say that the "fundamentals of our economy are strong."[3] But the fundamentals clearly were not strong and the line brought immediate criticism and ridicule, which forced McCain to backtrack. He looked unsteady on the economy, which became the nation's highest concern.

He and Obama had scheduled a debate for the end of September, but the financial crisis kept deepening. By then, Americans were panicked over the loss in value of their stocks, retirement accounts, and other assets. Polls showed they blamed the Bush administration, and by inference, McCain, as he represented Bush's Republican Party. McCain decided he had to do something drastic to show that he was on top of the situation. He decided to suspend his campaign and fly immediately to Washington, DC, to get involved with his fellow Senators and other members of Congress who were trying to come up with a rescue plan for the ailing financial firms.

McCain tried to get involved in the negotiations in Congress, but he found that the situation was complex and that his presence was not always helpful. Some people ignored him, others thought he was grandstanding. He found himself at odds over what to do even with some in his own party.

Then McCain made a mistake that while substantially minor, looked bad. He was scheduled to go on comedian David Letterman's late night television show just as he had suspended his campaigning. He called Letterman and cancelled, saying he had to get back to Washington. But he then gave an interview to Katie Couric of CBS News instead, leading Letterman to make fun of him, mocking him for saying he was going to go back to Washington when, in fact, he was getting his makeup on for the Couric interview. Letterman, apparently insulted, showed tape of the makeup session and made fun of McCain. McCain, who had always counted on favorable treatment from the late-night comedian's talk show, was stunned.

Reversing course again, McCain said he would debate Obama after all. Meanwhile, the financial bailout plan that McCain tried to help negotiate failed to pass through Congress. Many of his fellow Republicans voted against it. Congress would eventually pass a $700 billion package to help out the financial companies, but the damage to McCain's campaign had been done.

McCain performed well in the debates, particularly the last one where he felt more comfortable. Then a strange thing started to happen. The closer the campaign came to Election Day and the more the polls showed that he was going to lose, the more energized McCain became. He liked campaigning as the underdog.

McCain seized on a film clip of Obama talking to a plumber who was complaining about Obama's plan for higher taxes for wealthier Americans. "Joe the Plumber," as he came to be called (his real name is Samuel J. Wurzelbacher) maintained that by taxing his small business, Obama was being unfair. Obama said his point was to help lots of "Joes" to start their own businesses and to "spread the wealth around."[4] Conservatives latched onto that comment to brand Obama a socialist, and McCain started referring often to Joe the Plumber in his speeches to show that Obama wanted to hurt those who had begun to have financial success. It resonated with some partisan crowds but did not appear to be hurting Obama much.

Members of the campaign staff began sniping at each other, which is not unusual in losing campaigns when people want to place the blame elsewhere. But a lot of anonymous comments ended up in the newspapers and McCain seemed hurt that some in his campaign would be critical at this stage of the game. The anonymous aides were particularly critical of vice presidential candidate Sarah Palin, blaming her for bad interviews and gobbledegook on the campaign trail. There was a dustup over thousands of dollars in expensive clothes Palin had received, either from wealthy donors or the Republican Party, and it was never quite determined whether she returned some or all of the items.

McCain stopped talking to reporters on his plane and bus, going against all of his instincts that dealing with the press was a good thing. He campaigned from event to event but the inevitable was beginning to permeate his consciousness.

One positive highlight was McCain's last trip to Peterborough, New Hampshire, a small town where he previously had resurrected his campaigns in 1999 and earlier in 2008. It was a great town meeting—the old McCain was back, striding across the stage, taking questions (mostly friendly) from the thousands of supporters who had shown up to cheer him one more time.

"Thank you for your friendship," McCain said. "I came to say thank you, but I came to ask you for one more effort."[5]

But even New Hampshire would fail him this time. In the end, McCain won only 22 states, losing, in addition to New Hampshire, Republican stalwart states such as Indiana and North Carolina. McCain also lost battleground states such as Ohio, Florida, and Pennsylvania.

After the election, McCain would return to Washington as the Senator from Arizona and continue to work on his favorite issues—the Iraq War, immigration, international affairs, and campaign finance. He would be influential and sought after for his advice. Even a meeting with Obama, weeks after the election, went well (unlike in 2000 when it took him months to arrange a meeting with his rival George W. Bush). McCain seemed satisfied with the effort he had made, although not with the outcome.

In his concession speech, McCain urged all Americans to get behind him in supporting the new president, who, he said, would need all the help he could get in leading the country through economic and international crises. And, he blamed no one but himself for his loss.

"We fought as hard as we could. And though we fell short, the failure is mine, not yours," McCain told his supporters.[6]

He acknowledged the difficulties he had from the outset of the campaign such as running as a Republican, the same party to which the hugely unpopular George W. Bush belonged. But he said that with the help of his family and his campaign staff, he had done all he could.

> Tonight more than any night, I hold in my heart nothing
> but love for this country and for all its citizens whether they

supported me or Senator Obama. . . . I wish Godspeed to the man who was my former opponent and will be my president. And I call on all Americans, as I have often in this campaign, to not despair of our present difficulties, but to believe, always, in the promise and greatness of America, because nothing is inevitable here.

Americans never quit. We never surrender.

We never hide from history. We make history.

Thank you, and God Bless you and God bless America.[7]

NOTES

1. John McCain, speech, Arizona Biltmore Hotel and Resort, Phoenix, Arizona, November 4, 2008, www.nytimes.com/2008/11/04/us/politics/04text-mccain.html.

2. Ibid.

3. *Newsweek*, November 17, 2008, special election edition, p. 97, Vol. CLII, No. 20, Harlan, IA.

4. Larry Rohter and Liz Robbins, *The Caucus*, New York Times Politics Blog, "Joe in the Spotlight," October 16, 2008, http://thecaucus.blogs.nytimes.com/2008/10/16/joe-in-the-spotlight/.

5. Jill Zuckman, "John McCain's Lucky Charms," The Swamp blog, The Chicago Tribune's Washington Bureau, November 2, 2008, http://www.swamppolitics.com/news/politics/blog/2008/11/john_mccain_new_hampshire.html.

6. John McCain, speech, Arizona Biltmore Hotel and Resort, Phoenix, Arizona, November 4, 2008, www.nytimes.com/2008/11/04/us/politics/04text-mccain.html.

7. Ibid.

Appendix I

SPEECHES BY JOHN McCAIN

Thank you all very much. Tonight, I have a privilege given few Americans— the privilege of accepting our party's nomination for President of the United States. And I accept it with gratitude, humility and confidence.

In my life, no success has come without a good fight, and this nomination wasn't any different. That's a tribute to the candidates who opposed me and their supporters. They're leaders of great ability, who love our country, and wished to lead it to better days. Their support is an honor I won't forget.

I'm grateful to the President for leading us in those dark days following the worst attack on American soil in our history, and keeping us safe from another attack many thought was inevitable; and to the First Lady, Laura Bush, a model of grace and kindness in public and in private. And I'm grateful to the 41st President and his bride of 63 years, and for their outstanding example of honorable service to our country.

As always, I'm indebted to my wife, Cindy, and my seven children. The pleasures of family life can seem like a brief holiday from the crowded calendar of our nation's business. But I have treasured them all the more, and can't imagine a life without the happiness you give me. Cindy said a lot of nice things about me tonight. But, in truth, she's more my inspiration than I am hers. Her concern for those less blessed than we are—victims of land mines, children born in poverty and with birth defects—shows the measure of her humanity. I know she will make a great First Lady.

When I was growing up, my father was often at sea, and the job of raising my brother, sister and me would fall to my mother alone. Roberta Mc-Cain gave us her love of life, her deep interest in the world, her strength, and her belief we are all meant to use our opportunities to make ourselves useful to our country. I wouldn't be here tonight but for the strength of her character.

My heartfelt thanks to all of you, who helped me win this nomination, and stood by me when the odds were long. I won't let you down. To Americans who have yet to decide who to vote for, thank you for your consideration and the opportunity to win your trust. I intend to earn it.

Finally, a word to Senator Obama and his supporters. We'll go at it over the next two months. That's the nature of these contests, and there are big differences between us. But you have my respect and admiration. Despite our differences, much more unites us than divides us. We are fellow Americans, an association that means more to me than any other. We're dedicated to the proposition that all people are created equal and endowed by our Creator with inalienable rights. No country ever had a greater cause than that. And I wouldn't be an American worthy of the name if I didn't honor Senator Obama and his supporters for their achievement.

But let there be no doubt, my friends, we're going to win this election. And after we've won, we're going to reach out our hand to any willing patriot, make this government start working for you again, and get this country back on the road to prosperity and peace.

These are tough times for many of you. You're worried about keeping your job or finding a new one, and are struggling to put food on the table and stay in your home. All you ever asked of government is to stand on your side, not in your way. And that's just what I intend to do: stand on your side and fight for your future.

And I've found just the right partner to help me shake up Washington, Governor Sarah Palin of Alaska. She has executive experience and a real record of accomplishment. She's tackled tough problems like energy independence and corruption. She's balanced a budget, cut taxes, and taken on the special interests. She's reached across the aisle and asked Republicans, Democrats and Independents to serve in her administration. She's the mother of five children. She's helped run a small business, worked with her hands and knows what it's like to worry about mortgage payments and health care and the cost of gasoline and groceries.

She knows where she comes from and she knows who she works for. She stands up for what's right, and she doesn't let anyone tell her to sit down. I'm very proud to have introduced our next Vice President to the country. But I can't wait until I introduce her to Washington. And let me offer an advance warning to the old, big spending, do nothing, me first, country second Washington crowd: change is coming.

I'm not in the habit of breaking promises to my country and neither is Governor Palin. And when we tell you we're going to change Washington, and stop leaving our country's problems for some unluckier generation to fix, you can count on it. We've got a record of doing just that, and the strength, experience, judgment and backbone to keep our word to you.

You know, I've been called a maverick; someone who marches to the beat of his own drum. Sometimes it's meant as a compliment and sometimes it's not. What it really means is I understand who I work for. I don't work for a party. I don't work for a special interest. I don't work for myself. I work for you.

I've fought corruption, and it didn't matter if the culprits were Democrats or Republicans. They violated their public trust, and had to be held accountable. I've fought big spenders in both parties, who waste your money on things you neither need nor want, while you struggle to buy groceries, fill your gas tank and make your mortgage payment. I've fought to get million dollar checks out of our elections. I've fought lobbyists who stole from Indian tribes. I fought crooked deals in the Pentagon. I fought tobacco companies and trial lawyers, drug companies and union bosses.

I fought for the right strategy and more troops in Iraq, when it wasn't a popular thing to do. And when the pundits said my campaign was finished, I said I'd rather lose an election than see my country lose a war.

Thanks to the leadership of a brilliant general, David Petreaus, and the brave men and women he has the honor to command, that strategy succeeded and rescued us from a defeat that would have demoralized our military, risked a wider war and threatened the security of all Americans.

I don't mind a good fight. For reasons known only to God, I've had quite a few tough ones in my life. But I learned an important lesson along the way. In the end, it matters less that you can fight. What you fight for is the real test.

I fight for Americans. I fight for you. I fight for Bill and Sue Nebe from Farmington Hills, Michigan, who lost their real estate investments in the bad housing market. Bill got a temporary job after he was out of work for seven months. Sue works three jobs to help pay the bills.

I fight for Jake and Toni Wimmer of Franklin County, Pennsylvania. Jake works on a loading dock, coaches Little League, and raises money for the mentally and physically disabled. Toni is a schoolteacher, working toward her Master's Degree. They have two sons; the youngest, Luke, has been diagnosed with autism. Their lives should matter to the people they elect to office. They matter to me.

I fight for the family of Matthew Stanley of Wolfboro, New Hampshire, who died serving our country in Iraq. I wear his bracelet and think of him every day. I intend to honor their sacrifice by making sure the country their son loved so well and never returned to, remains safe from its enemies.

I fight to restore the pride and principles of our party. We were elected to change Washington, and we let Washington change us. We lost the trust of the American people when some Republicans gave in to the temptations of corruption. We lost their trust when rather than reform government, both parties made it bigger. We lost their trust when instead of freeing ourselves from a dangerous dependence on foreign oil, both parties and Senator Obama passed another corporate welfare bill for oil companies. We lost their trust, when we valued our power over our principles.

We're going to change that. We're going to recover the people's trust by standing up again for the values Americans admire. The party of Lincoln, Roosevelt and Reagan is going to get back to basics.

We believe everyone has something to contribute and deserves the opportunity to reach their God-given potential from the boy whose descendents arrived on the Mayflower to the Latina daughter of migrant workers. We're all God's children and we're all Americans.

We believe in low taxes, spending discipline, and open markets. We believe in rewarding hard work and risk takers and letting people keep the fruits of their labor.

We believe in a strong defense, work, faith, service, a culture of life, personal responsibility, the rule of law, and judges who dispense justice impartially and don't legislate from the bench. We believe in the values of families, neighborhoods and communities.

We believe in a government that unleashes the creativity and initiative of Americans. Government that doesn't make your choices for you, but works to make sure you have more choices to make for yourself.

I will keep taxes low and cut them where I can. My opponent will raise them. I will open new markets to our goods and services. My opponent will close them. I will cut government spending. He will increase it.

My tax cuts will create jobs. His tax increases will eliminate them. My health care plan will make it easier for more Americans to find and keep good health care insurance. His plan will force small businesses to cut jobs, reduce wages, and force families into a government run health care system where a bureaucrat stands between you and your doctor.

Keeping taxes low helps small businesses grow and create new jobs. Cutting the second highest business tax rate in the world will help American companies compete and keep jobs from moving overseas. Doubling the child tax exemption from $3,500 to $7,000 will improve the lives of millions of American families. Reducing government spending and getting rid of failed programs will let you keep more of your own money to save, spend and invest as you see fit. Opening new markets and preparing workers to compete in the world economy is essential to our future prosperity.

I know some of you have been left behind in the changing economy and it often seems your government hasn't even noticed. Government assistance for unemployed workers was designed for the economy of the 1950s. That's going to change on my watch. My opponent promises to bring back old jobs by wishing away the global economy. We're going to help workers who've lost a job that won't come back, find a new one that won't go away.

We will prepare them for the jobs of today. We will use our community colleges to help train people for new opportunities in their communities. For workers in industries that have been hard hit, we'll help make up part of the difference in wages between their old job and a temporary, lower paid one while they receive retraining that will help them find secure new employment at a decent wage.

Education is the civil rights issue of this century. Equal access to public education has been gained. But what is the value of access to a failing school? We need to shake up failed school bureaucracies with competition, empower parents with choice, remove barriers to qualified instructors, attract and reward good teachers, and help bad teachers find another line of work.

When a public school fails to meet its obligations to students, parents deserve a choice in the education of their children. And I intend to give it to them. Some may choose a better public school. Some may choose a private one. Many will choose a charter school. But they will have that choice and their children will have that opportunity.

Senator Obama wants our schools to answer to unions and entrenched bureaucracies. I want schools to answer to parents and students. And when I'm President, they will.

My fellow Americans, when I'm President, we're going to embark on the most ambitious national project in decades. We are going to stop sending $700 billion a year to countries that don't like us very much. We will attack the problem on every front. We will produce more energy at home. We will drill new wells offshore, and we'll drill them now.

We will build more nuclear power plants. We will develop clean coal technology. We will increase the use of wind, tide, solar and natural gas. We will encourage the development and use of flex fuel, hybrid and electric automobiles.

Senator Obama thinks we can achieve energy independence without more drilling and without more nuclear power. But Americans know better than that. We must use all resources and develop all technologies necessary to rescue our economy from the damage caused by rising oil prices and to restore the health of our planet. It's an ambitious plan, but Americans are ambitious by nature, and we have faced greater challenges. It's time for us to show the world again how Americans lead.

This great national cause will create millions of new jobs, many in industries that will be the engine of our future prosperity; jobs that will be there when your children enter the workforce.

Today, the prospect of a better world remains within our reach. But we must see the threats to peace and liberty in our time clearly and face them, as Americans before us did, with confidence, wisdom and resolve.

We have dealt a serious blow to al Qaeda in recent years. But they are not defeated, and they'll strike us again if they can. Iran remains the chief state sponsor of terrorism and on the path to acquiring nuclear weapons. Russia's leaders, rich with oil wealth and corrupt with power, have rejected democratic ideals and the obligations of a responsible power. They invaded a small, democratic neighbor to gain more control over the world's oil supply, intimidate other neighbors, and further their ambitions of reassembling the Russian empire. And the brave people of Georgia need our solidarity and prayers. As President I will work to establish good relations with Russia so we need not fear a return of the Cold War. But we can't turn a blind eye to aggression and international lawlessness that threatens the peace and stability of the world and the security of the American people.

We face many threats in this dangerous world, but I'm not afraid of them. I'm prepared for them. I know how the military works, what it can do, what it can do better, and what it should not do. I know how the world works. I know the good and the evil in it. I know how to work with leaders who share our dreams of a freer, safer and more prosperous world, and how to stand up to those who don't. I know how to secure the peace.

When I was five years old, a car pulled up in front of our house. A Navy officer rolled down the window, and shouted at my father that the Japanese had bombed Pearl Harbor. I rarely saw my father again for four years. My grandfather came home from that same war exhausted from the burdens he had borne, and died the next day. In Vietnam, where I formed the closest friendships of my life, some of those friends never came home with me. I hate war. It is terrible beyond imagination.

I'm running for President to keep the country I love safe, and prevent other families from risking their loved ones in war as my family has. I will draw on all my experience with the world and its leaders, and all the tools at our disposal—diplomatic, economic, military and the power of our ideals—to build the foundations for a stable and enduring peace.

In America, we change things that need to be changed. Each generation makes its contribution to our greatness. The work that is ours to do is plainly before us. We don't need to search for it.

We need to change the way government does almost everything: from the way we protect our security to the way we compete in the world economy; from the way we respond to disasters to the way we fuel our transportation network; from the way we train our workers to the way we educate our children. All these functions of government were designed before the rise of the global economy, the information technology revolution and the end of the Cold War. We have to catch up to history, and we have to change the way we do business in Washington.

The constant partisan rancor that stops us from solving these problems isn't a cause, it's a symptom. It's what happens when people go to Washington to work for themselves and not you.

Again and again, I've worked with members of both parties to fix problems that need to be fixed. That's how I will govern as President. I will reach out my hand to anyone to help me get this country moving again. I have that record and the scars to prove it. Senator Obama does not.

Instead of rejecting good ideas because we didn't think of them first, let's use the best ideas from both sides. Instead of fighting over who gets the credit, let's try sharing it. This amazing country can do anything we put our minds to. I will ask Democrats and Independents to serve with me. And my administration will set a new standard for transparency and accountability.

We're going to finally start getting things done for the people who are counting on us, and I won't care who gets the credit.

I've been an imperfect servant of my country for many years. But I have been her servant first, last and always. And I've never lived a day, in good times or bad, that I didn't thank God for the privilege.

Long ago, something unusual happened to me that taught me the most valuable lesson of my life. I was blessed by misfortune. I mean that sincerely. I was blessed because I served in the company of heroes, and I witnessed a thousand acts of courage, compassion and love.

On an October morning, in the Gulf of Tonkin, I prepared for my 23rd mission over North Vietnam. I hadn't any worry I wouldn't come back safe and sound. I thought I was tougher than anyone. I was pretty independent then, too. I liked to bend a few rules, and pick a few fights for the fun of it. But I did it for my own pleasure; my own pride. I didn't think there was a cause more important than me.

Then I found myself falling toward the middle of a small lake in the city of Hanoi, with two broken arms, a broken leg, and an angry crowd waiting to greet me. I was dumped in a dark cell, and left to die. I didn't feel so tough anymore. When they discovered my father was an admiral, they took me to a hospital. They couldn't set my bones properly, so they just slapped a cast on me. When I didn't get better, and was down to about a hundred pounds, they put me in a cell with two other Americans. I couldn't do anything. I couldn't even feed myself. They did it for me. I was beginning to learn the limits of my selfish independence. Those men saved my life.

I was in solitary confinement when my captors offered to release me. I knew why. If I went home, they would use it as propaganda to demoralize my fellow prisoners. Our Code said we could only go home in the order of our capture, and there were men who had been shot down before me. I thought about it, though. I wasn't in great shape, and I missed everything about America. But I turned it down.

A lot of prisoners had it worse than I did. I'd been mistreated before, but not as badly as others. I always liked to strut a little after I'd been roughed up to show the other guys I was tough enough to take it. But after I turned down their offer, they worked me over harder than they ever had before. For a long time. And they broke me.

When they brought me back to my cell, I was hurt and ashamed, and I didn't know how I could face my fellow prisoners. The good man in the cell next door, my friend, Bob Craner, saved me. Through taps on a wall he told me I had fought as hard as I could. No man can always stand alone. And then he told me to get back up and fight again for our country and for the men I had the honor to serve with. Because every day they fought for me.

I fell in love with my country when I was a prisoner in someone else's. I loved it not just for the many comforts of life here. I loved it for its decency; for its faith in the wisdom, justice and goodness of its people. I loved it because it was not just a place, but an idea, a cause worth fighting for. I was never the same again. I wasn't my own man anymore. I was my country's.

I'm not running for president because I think I'm blessed with such personal greatness that history has anointed me to save our country in its hour of need. My country saved me. My country saved me, and I cannot forget it. And I will fight for her for as long as I draw breath, so help me God.

If you find faults with our country, make it a better one. If you're disappointed with the mistakes of government, join its ranks and work to correct them. Enlist in our Armed Forces. Become a teacher. Enter the ministry. Run for public office. Feed a hungry child. Teach an illiterate adult to read. Comfort the afflicted. Defend the rights of the oppressed. Our country will be the better, and you will be the happier. Because nothing brings greater happiness in life than to serve a cause greater than yourself.

I'm going to fight for my cause every day as your President. I'm going to fight to make sure every American has every reason to thank God, as I thank Him: that I'm an American, a proud citizen of the greatest country on earth, and with hard work, strong faith and a little courage, great things are always within our reach. Fight with me. Fight with me.

Fight for what's right for our country.

Fight for the ideals and character of a free people.

Fight for our children's future.

Fight for justice and opportunity for all.

Stand up to defend our country from its enemies.

Stand up for each other; for beautiful, blessed, bountiful America.

Stand up, stand up, stand up and fight. Nothing is inevitable here. We're Americans, and we never give up. We never quit. We never hide from history. We make history.

Thank you, and God bless you.

SPEECH ON CLINCHING THE REPUBLICAN NOMINATION FOR PRESIDENT

February 19, 2008, Dallas, Texas

Thank you, my friends, for your support and dedication to our campaign. And thank you, Wisconsin, for bringing us to the point when even a superstitious naval aviator can claim with confidence and humility that I will be our party's nominee for President. I promise you, I will wage a campaign with determination, passion and the right ideas for strengthening our country that prove worthy of the honor and responsibility you have given me.

I, again, want to commend Governor Huckabee, who has shown impressive grit and passion himself, and whom, though he remains my opponent, I have come to admire very much. And, of course, I want to thank my wife, Cindy, and my daughter, Meghan, who are here tonight, and the rest of my family for their indispensable love and encouragement.

My friends, we have traveled a great distance together already in this campaign, and overcome more than a few obstacles. But as I said last week, now comes the hard part and, for America, the bigger decision. Will we make the right changes to restore the people's trust in their government and meet the great challenges of our time with wisdom, and with faith in the values and ability of Americans for whom no challenge is greater than their resolve, courage and patriotism? Or will we heed appeals for change that ignore the lessons of history, and lack confidence in the intelligence and ideals of free people?

I will fight every moment of every day in this campaign to make sure Americans are not deceived by an eloquent but empty call for change that promises no more than a holiday from history and a return to the false promises and failed policies of a tired philosophy that trusts in government more than people. Our purpose is to keep this blessed country free, safe, prosperous and proud. And the changes we offer to the institutions and policies of government will reflect and rely upon the strength, industry, aspirations and decency of the people we serve.

We live in a world of change, some of which holds great promise for us and all mankind and some of which poses great peril. Today, political change in Pakistan is occurring that might affect our relationship with a nuclear armed nation that is indispensable to our success in combating al Qaeda in Afghanistan and elsewhere. An old enemy of American interests and ideals is leaving the world stage, and we can glimpse the hope that freedom might someday come to the people of Cuba. A self-important bully in Venezuela threatens to cut off oil shipments to our country at a time of sky-rocketing gas prices. Each event poses a challenge and an opportunity. Will the next President have the experience, the judgment experience informs, and the strength of purpose to respond to each of these developments in ways that strengthen our security and advance the global progress of our ideals? Or will we risk the confused leadership of an inexperienced candidate who once suggested invading our ally, Pakistan, and sitting down without pre-conditions or clear purpose with enemies who support terrorists and are intent on destabilizing the world by acquiring nuclear weapons?

The most important obligation of the next President is to protect Americans from the threat posed by violent extremists who despise us, our values and modernity itself. They are moral monsters, but they are also a disciplined, dedicated movement driven by an apocalyptic zeal, which celebrates murder, has access to science, technology and mass communications, and is determined to acquire and use against us weapons of mass destruction. The institutions and doctrines we relied on in the Cold War are no longer adequate to protect us in a struggle where suicide bombers might obtain the world's most terrifying weapons.

If we are to succeed, we must rethink and rebuild the structure and mission of our military; the capabilities of our intelligence and law enforcement agencies; the purposes of our alliances; the reach and scope of our diplomacy; the capacity of all branches of government to defend us. We need to marshal all elements of American power: our military, economy, investment, trade and technology and our moral credibility to win the war against Islamic extremists and help the majority of Muslims, who believe in progress and peace, win the struggle for the soul of Islam.

The challenges and opportunities of the global economy require us to change some old habits of our government as well. But we will fight for the right changes; changes that understand our strengths and rely on the common sense and values of the American people. We will campaign:

— to balance the federal budget not with smoke and mirrors, but by encouraging economic growth and preventing government from spending your money on things it shouldn't; to hold it accountable for the money it does spend on services that only government can provide in ways that don't fail and embarrass you;

— to save Social Security and Medicare on our watch without the tricks, lies and posturing that have failed us for too long while the problem became harder to solve;

— to make our tax code simpler, fairer, flatter, more pro-growth and pro-jobs;

— to reduce our dangerous dependence on foreign oil with an energy policy that encourages American industry and technology to make our country safer, cleaner and more prosperous by leading the world in the use, development and discovery of alternative sources of energy;

— to open new markets to American goods and services, create more and better jobs for the American worker and overhaul unemployment insurance and our redundant and outmoded programs for assisting workers who have lost a job that's not coming back to find a job that won't go away;

— to help Americans without health insurance acquire it without bankrupting the country, and ruining the quality of American health care that is the envy of the world;

— to make our public schools more accountable to parents and better able to meet the critical responsibility they have to prepare our children for the challenges they'll face in the world they'll lead.

I'm not the youngest candidate. But I am the most experienced. I know what our military can do, what it can do better, and what it should not do. I know how Congress works, and how to make it work for the country and not just the re-election of its members. I know how the world works. I know the good and the evil in it. I know how to work with leaders who share our dreams of a freer, safer and more prosperous world, and how to stand up to those who don't. And I know who I am and what I want to do.

I don't seek the office out of a sense of entitlement. I owe America more than she has ever owed me. I have been an imperfect servant of my country for many years. I have never lived a day, in good times or bad, that I haven't been proud of the privilege. Don't tell me what we can't do. Don't tell me we can't make our country stronger and the world safer. We can. We must. And when I'm President we will.

Thank you, and God bless you.

SPEECH ON WINNING THE NEW HAMPSHIRE REPUBLICAN PRIMARY

January 8, 2008, Manchester, New Hampshire

Thank you.

My friends, I am past the age when I can claim the noun "kid," no matter what adjective precedes it. But tonight we sure showed them what a comeback looks like. When the pundits declared us finished, I told them, "I'm going to New Hampshire, where the voters don't let you make their decision for them." And when they asked, "How are you going to do it? You're down in the polls. You don't have the money," I answered, "I'm going to New Hampshire, and I'm going to tell people the truth."

We came back here to this wonderful state we've come to trust and love. And we had just one strategy: to tell you what I believe. I didn't just tell you what the polls said you wanted to hear. I didn't tell you what I knew to be false. I didn't try to spin you. I just talked to the people of New Hampshire. I talked about the country we love; the many challenges we face together; and the great promise that is ours to achieve; the work that awaits us in this hour, on our watch: to defend our country from its enemies; to advance the ideals that are our greatest strength; to increase the prosperity and opportunities of all Americans and to make in our time, as each preceding American generation has, another, better world than the one we inherited.

I talked to the people of New Hampshire. I reasoned with you. I listened to you. I answered you. Sometimes, I argued with you. But I always told you the truth, as best as I can see the truth. And you did me the great honor of listening. Thank you, New Hampshire, from the bottom my heart. I am grateful and humbled and more certain than ever that before I can win your vote, I must win your respect. And I must do that by being honest with you, and then put my trust in your fairness and good judgment.

Tonight, we have taken a step, but only the first step toward repairing the broken politics of the past and restoring the trust of the American people in their government. The people of New Hampshire have told us again that they do not send us to Washington to serve our self-interest, but to serve theirs. They don't send us to fight each other for our own political ambitions; but to fight together our real enemies. They don't send us to Washington to stroke our egos; but to help them keep this beautiful, bountiful, blessed country safe, prosperous and proud. They don't send us to Washington to take more of their money, and waste it on things that add not an ounce to America's strength and prosperity; that don't help a single family realize the dreams we all dream for our children; that don't help a single displaced worker find a new job, and the security and dignity it assures them; that won't keep the promise we make to young workers that the retirement they have begun to invest in, will be there for them when they need it. They don't send us to Washington to do their job, but to do ours.

My friends, I didn't go to Washington to go along, to get along or to play it safe to serve my own interests. I went there to serve my country. And that, my friends, is just what I intend to do if I am so privileged to be elected your President.

I seek the nomination of a party that believes in the strength, industry, and goodness of the American people. We don't believe that government has all the answers, but that it should respect the rights, property and opportunities of the people to whom we are accountable. We don't believe in growing the size of government to make it easier to serve our own ambitions. But what government is expected to do, it must do with competence, resolve and wisdom. In recent years, we have lost the trust of the people, who share our principles, but doubt our own allegiance to them. I seek the nomination of our party to restore that trust; to return our party to the principles that have never failed Americans: The party of fiscal discipline, low taxes; enduring values; a strong and capable defense; that encourages the enterprise and ingenuity of individuals, businesses and families, who know best how to advance America's economy, and secure the dreams that have made us the greatest nation in history.

The work that we face in our time is great, but our opportunities greater still. In a time of war, and the terrible sacrifices it entails, the promise of a better future is not always clear. But I promise you, my friends, we face no enemy, no matter how cruel; and no challenge, no matter how daunting, greater than the courage, patriotism and determination of Americans. We are the makers of history, not its victims. And as we confront this enemy, the people privileged to serve in public office should not evade our mutual responsibility to defeat them because we are more concerned with personal or partisan ambition. Whatever the differences between us, so much more should unite us. And nothing should unite us more closely than the imperative of defeating an enemy who despises us, our values and modernity itself. We must all pull together in this critical hour and proclaim that the history of the world will not be determined by this unpardonable foe, but by the aspirations, ideals, faith and courage of free people. In this great, historic task, we will never surrender. They will.

The results of the other party's primary is uncertain at this time, but I want to congratulate all the campaigns in both parties. I salute the supporters of all the candidates who worked so hard to achieve a success tonight and who believe so passionately in the promise of their candidate. And I want to assure them that though I did not have their support, and though we may disagree from time to time on how best to advance America's interests and ideals, they have my genuine respect. For they have worked for a cause they believe is good for the country we all love, a cause greater than their self-interest.

I learned long ago that serving only oneself is a petty and unsatisfying ambition. But serve a cause greater than self-interest and you will know a happiness far more sublime than the fleeting pleasure of fame and fortune. For me that greater cause has always been my country, which I have served imperfectly for many years, but have loved without any reservation every day of my life. And however this campaign turns out—and I am more confident tonight that it will turn out much better than once expected—I am grateful beyond expression for the prospect that I might serve her a little while longer. That gratitude imposes on me the responsibility to do nothing in this campaign that would make our country's problems harder to solve or that would cause Americans to despair that a candidate for the highest office in the land would think so little of the honor that he would put his own interests before theirs. I take that responsibility as my most solemn trust.

So, my friends, we celebrate one victory tonight and leave for Michigan tomorrow to win another. But let us remember that our purpose is not ours alone; our success is not an end in itself. America is our cause—yesterday, today, and tomorrow. Her greatness is our hope; her strength is our protection; her ideals our greatest treasure; her prosperity the promise we keep to our children; her goodness the hope of mankind. That is the cause of our campaign and the platform of my party, and I will stay true to it so help me God.

Thank you, New Hampshire. Thank you, my friends, and God bless you as you have blessed me. Enjoy this. You have earned it more than me. Tomorrow, we begin again.

SPEECH TO THE 2000 REPUBLICAN CONVENTION

August 1, 2000, Philadelphia, Pennsylvania

I am grateful for your kindness to a distant runner-up. And I am proud to join you this evening in commending to all Americans the man who now represents your best wishes and mine for the future of our country, my friend, Governor George W. Bush, the next President of the United States.

Tomorrow, we will formally nominate Governor Bush. We do so not for our sake alone. We do not seek his election merely to acquire an advantage over our political opponents or offices for our party faithful. We have a grander purpose than that.

When we nominate Governor Bush for President, here in the city where our great nation was born, we invest him with the faith of our founding fathers, and charge him with the care of the cause they called glorious.

We are blessed to be Americans, not just in times of prosperity, but at all times. We are part of something providential; a great experiment to prove to the world that democracy is not only the most effective form of government, but the only moral government. And through the years, generation after generation of Americans has held fast to the belief that we were meant to transform history.

On an early December morning, many years ago, I watched my father leave for war. He joined millions of Americans to fight a world war that would decide the fate of humanity. They fought against a cruel and formidable enemy bent on world domination. They fought not just for themselves and their families, not just to preserve the quality of their own lives. They fought for love, for love of an idea—that America stood for something greater than the sum of our individual interests.

From where did the courage come to make the maximum effort in that decisive moment in history? It marched with the sons of a nation that believed deeply in itself, in its history, in the justice of its cause, in its magnificent destiny. Americans went into battle armed against despair with the common conviction that the country that had sent them there was worth their sacrifice.

Their families, their schools, their faith, their history, their heroes taught them that the freedom with which they were blessed deserved patriots to defend it.

Many would never come home. But those who did returned with an even deeper civic love. They believed that if America were worth dying for, then surely she was worth living for. They were, as Tocqueville said of Americans, "united by visions of what will be."

They built an even greater nation than the one they had left their homes to defend; an America that offered more opportunities to more of its people than ever before; an America that began to redress injustices that had been visited on too many of her citizens for too long. They bound up the wounds of war for ally and enemy alike. And when faced with a new, terrible threat to the security and freedom of the world, they fought that too. As did their sons and daughters. And they prevailed.

An Age of Untold Possibilities

Now we stand unsurpassed in our wealth and power. What shall we make of it? Let us take courage from their example, and from the new world they built, build a better one.

This new century will be an age of untold possibilities for us and for all mankind. Many nations now share our love of liberty and aspire to the ordered progress of democracy. But the world is still home to tyrants, haters and aggressors hostile to America and our ideals. We are obliged to seize this moment to help build a safer, freer and more prosperous world, completely free of the tyranny that made the last century such a violent age.

We are strong, confident people. We know that our ideals, our courage, our ingenuity ensure our success. Isolationism and protectionism are fool's errands. We shouldn't build walls to the global success of our interests and values. Walls are for cowards, my friends, not for Americans. No nation complacent in its greatness will long sustain it. We are an unfinished nation. And we are not a people of half-measures. We who have found shelter beneath the great oak must care for it in our time with as much devotion as had the patriots who preceded us.

This is an extraordinary time to be alive. We are so strong and prosperous that we can scarcely imagine the heights we could ascend if we have the will to make the climb. Yet I think each of us senses that America, for all our prosperity, is in danger of losing the best sense of herself: that there is a purpose to being an American beyond materialism.

Cynicism is suffocating the idealism of many Americans, especially among our young. And with cause, for they have lost pride in their government.

A Part of Something Greater

Too often those who hold a public trust have failed to set the necessary example. Too often, partisanship seems all consuming. Differences are defined with derision. Too often, we seem to put our personal interests before the national interest, leaving the people's business unattended while we posture, poll and spin. When the people believe that government no longer embodies our founding ideals, then basic civil consensus will deteriorate as people seek substitutes for the unifying values of patriotism. National pride will not endure the people's contempt for government. And national pride is as indispensable to the happiness of Americans as is our self-respect.

When we quit seeing ourselves as part of something greater than our self-interest then civic love gives way to the temptations of selfishness, bigotry and hate. Unless we restore the people's sovereignty over government, renew their pride in public service, reform our public institutions to meet the challenges of a new day and reinvigorate our national purpose then America's best days will be behind us.

To achieve the necessary changes to the practices and institutions of our democracy we need to be a little less content. We need to get riled up a bit, and stand up for the values that made America great.

Rally to this new patriotic challenge or lose forever America's extraordinary ability to see around the corner of history. Americans, enter the public life of your country determined to tell the truth; to put problem solving ahead of partisanship; to defend the national interest against the forces that would divide us. Keep your promise to America, as she has kept her promise to you, and you will know a happiness far more sublime than pleasure.

It is easy to forget in politics where principle ends and selfishness begins. It takes leaders of courage and character to remember the difference.

Tomorrow, our party will nominate such a leader. George W. Bush believes in the greatness of America and the justice of our cause. He believes in the America of the immigrant's dream, the high lantern of freedom and hope to the world. He is proud of America's stature as the world's only superpower, and he accepts the responsibilities along with the blessings that come with that hard-earned distinction. He knows well that there is no safe alternative to American leadership. And he will not squander this unique moment in history by allowing America to retreat behind empty threats, false promises, and uncertain diplomacy. He will confidently defend our interests and values wherever they are threatened.

An Ennobling Person

I say to all Americans, Republican, Democrat or Independent, if you believe America deserves leaders with a purpose more ennobling than expediency and opportunism, then vote for Governor Bush. If you believe patriotism is more than a soundbite and public service should be more than a photo-op then vote for Governor Bush.

My friend, Governor Bush, believes in an America that is so much more than the sum of its divided parts. He wants to give you back a government that serves all the people no matter the circumstances of their birth. And he wants to lead a Republican Party that is as big as the country we serve.

He wants nothing to divide us into separate nations. Not our color. Not our race. Not our wealth. Not our religion. Not our politics. He wants us to live for America, as one nation, and together profess the American Creed of self-evident truths.

I support him. I am grateful to him. And I am proud of him.

He is a good man from a good family that has, in good times and bad, dedicated themselves to America. Many years ago, the Governor's father served in the Pacific, with distinction, under the command of my grandfather. Now it is my turn to serve under the son of my grandfather's brave subordinate.

I am proud to do so for I know that by supporting George W. Bush I serve my country well.

America's Rise to Prominence

My grandfather was an aviator; my father a submariner. They gave their lives to their country. In Tokyo Harbor, on the day the Japanese surrendered, they were re-united for the last time. My grandfather would die a few days later. His last words to my father were "it's an honor to die for your country and your principles." I have been an imperfect servant of my country for over forty years, and my many mistakes rightly humble me. But I am their son . . . and they taught me to love my country, and that has made all the difference, my friends, all the difference in the world.

I am so grateful to have seen America rise to such prominence. But America's greatness is a quest without end, the object beyond the horizon. And it is an inescapable and bittersweet irony of life, that the older we are the more distant the horizon becomes. I will not see what is over America's horizon. The years that remain are not too few I trust, but the immortality that was the aspiration of my youth, has, like all the treasures of youth, quietly slipped away.

But I have faith. I have faith in you. I have faith in your patriotism, in your passion to build upon the accomplishments of our storied past. I have faith that people who are free to act in their own interests will perceive their interests in an enlightened way and live as one nation, in a kinship of ideals, served by a government that kindles the pride of every one of you.

I have faith that just beyond the distant horizon live a people who gratefully accept the obligation of their freedom to make of their power and wealth a civilization for the ages—a civilization in which all people share in the promise of freedom.

I have such faith in you, my fellow Americans.

And I am united by the vision of what will be.

EXCERPTS FROM SPEECH ON WITHDRAWING FROM THE 2000 PRESIDENTIAL CAMPAIGN

March 10, 2000, Sedona, Arizona

We knew when we began this campaign that ours was a difficult challenge.

Last Tuesday that challenge became considerably more difficult as a majority of Republican voters made clear their preference for president is Governor Bush. I respect their decision. And I'm truly grateful for the distinct privilege of even being considered for the highest office in this, the greatest nation in the history of mankind.

Therefore I announce today, on this fine Arizona morning and in this beautiful place, that I am no longer an active candidate for my party's nomination for president.

I congratulate Governor Bush and wish him and his family well. He may very well become the next president of the United States. That is an honor accorded to very few and is such a great responsibility that he deserves the best wishes of every American. He certainly has mine.

I'm suspending my campaign so that Cindy and I can take some time to reflect on our recent experiences and determine how we can best continue to serve the country and help bring about the changes to the practices and institutions of our great democracy that are the purpose of our campaign. . . .

I hoped our campaign would be a force for change in the Republican Party, and I believe we have, indeed, set a course that will ultimately prevail in making our party as big as the country we serve.

Millions of Americans have rallied to our banner. And their support not just honors me, but has ignited the cause of reform, a cause far greater and more important than the ambitions of any single candidate.

I love my party. It is my home. Ours is the party of Lincoln, Roosevelt and Reagan. That's good company for any American to keep. And it is a distinct privilege to serve the same cause that those great Americans dedicated their lives to.

But I'm also dedicated to the necessary cause of reform. And I will never walk away from a fight for what I know is right and just for our country.

As I said throughout the campaign, what is good for my country is good for my party. Should our party ever abandon this principle, the American people will rightly abandon us and we will surely slip into the mists of history, deserving the allegiance of none.

So I will take our crusade back to the United States Senate. And I will keep fighting to save the government—to give the government back to the people, to keep our promises to young and old alike by paying our debts, saving Social Security and Medicare and reforming a tax code that benefits the powerful few at the expense of many.

And with your help, my fellow Americans, we will keep trying to force open doors where there are walls to your full participation in the great enterprises of our democracy, be they walls of cynicism or intolerance or walls raised by self-interested elite who would exclude your voice from the highest councils of our government.

I want to take a final moment to speak to all those who joined our party to support our campaign, many of whom voted in this election for the first time. Thank you. Thank you from the bottom of my heart. Your support means more to me than I can ever say.

But I ask from you one last promise: Promise me that you will never give up, that you will continue your service in the worthy cause of revitalizing our democracy. . . .

You served your country in this campaign by fighting for the causes that will sustain America's greatness. Keep fighting, my friends, keep fighting. America needs you.

Thank you, my friends. Thank you so much for helping me remember what it means to be a public servant in this, the most blessed and most important nation on earth.

It has been the greatest privilege of my life.

Appendix II

U.S. Presidential Elections Since 1860 (Major Candidates)

Presidential Candidates	Party	Votes (%)	Electoral College (%)	Vice Presidential Candidates	Party
		1860 - 11/06/1860			
Abraham Lincoln	Republican	1,855,993 (39.65)	180 (59.41)	**Hannibal Hamlin**	Republican
John Breckenridge	Democratic	851,844 (18.20)	72 (23.76)	Joseph Lane	Democratic
		1864 - 11/08/1864			
Abraham Lincoln	Union	2,211,317 (55.03)	212 (90.99)	**Andrew Johnson**	Union
George McClellan	Democratic	1,806,227 (44.95)	21 (9.01)	G.H. Pendleton	Democratic
		1868 - 11/03/1868			
Ulysses Grant	Republican	3,013,790 (52.66)	214 (72.79)	**Schuyler Colfax**	Republican
Horatio Seymour	Democratic	2,708,980 (47.34)	80 (27.21)	Francis Blair	Democratic
		1872 - 11/05/1872			
Ulysses Grant	Republican	3,597,439 (55.58)	286 (81.25)	**Henry Wilson**	Republican
Horace Greeley[1]	Democratic, Liberal Republicans	2,833,710 (43.78)	0 (0.00)	B. Gratz Brown	Democratic, Liberal Republicans

(*continued*)

U.S. Presidential Elections Since 1860 (Major Candidates) (*continued*)

Presidential Candidates	Party	Votes (%)	Electoral College (%)	Vice Presidential Candidates	Party
1876 - 11/07/1876					
Rutherford Hayes	Republican	4,034,142 (47.92)	185 (50.14)	**William Wheeler**	Republican
Samuel Tilden	Democratic	4,286,808 (50.92)	184 (49.86)	Thomas Hendricks	Democratic
1880 - 11/02/1880					
James Garfield	Republican	4,453,337 (48.31)	214 (57.99)	**Chester Arthur**	Republican
Winfield Hancock	Democratic	4,444,267 (48.22)	155 (42.01)	William English	Democratic
1884 - 11/04/1884					
Grover Cleveland	Democratic	4,914,482 (48.85)	219 (54.61)	**Thomas Hendricks**	Democratic
James Blaine	Republican	4,856,903 (48.28)	182 (45.39)	John Logan	Republican
1888 - 11/06/1888					
Benjamin Harrison	Republican	5,443,633 (47.80)	233 (58.10)	**Levi Morton**	Republican
Grover Cleveland	Democratic	5,538,163 (48.63)	168 (41.90)	A.G. Thurman	Democratic
1892 - 11/08/1892					
Grover Cleveland	Democratic	5,553,898 (46.02)	277 (62.39)	**Adlai Stevenson**	Democratic
Benjamin Harrison	Republican	5,190,799 (43.01)	145 (32.66)	Whitelaw Reid	Republican
James Weaver	People's	1,026,595 (8.51)	22 (4.95)	James Field	People's
1896 - 11/03/1896					
William McKinley	Republican	7,112,138 (51.02)	271 (60.63)	**Garret Hobart**	Republican
William Bryan	Democratic, People's	6,510,807 (46.71)	176 (39.37)	Arthur Sewall	Democratic
				Thomas Watson	People's

U.S. Presidential Elections Since 1860 (Major Candidates) (*continued*)

Presidential Candidates	Party	Votes (%)	Electoral College (%)	Vice Presidential Candidates	Party
		1900 - 11/06/1900			
William McKinley	Republican	7,228,864 (51.64)	292 (65.32)	**Theodore Roosevelt**	Republican
William Bryan	Democratic, People's	6,370,932 (45.52)	155 (34.68)	Adlai Stevenson	Democratic, People's
		1904 - 11/08/1904			
Theodore Roosevelt	Republican	7,630,557 (56.42)	336 (70.59)	**Charles Fairbanks**	Republican
Alton Parker	Democratic	5,083,880 (37.59)	140 (29.41)	Henry Davis	Democratic
		1908 - 11/03/1908			
William Taft	Republican	7,678,335 (51.57)	321 (66.46)	**James Sherman**	Republican
William Bryan	Democratic	6,408,979 (43.04)	162 (33.54)	John Kern	Democratic
		1912 - 11/05/1912			
Woodrow Wilson	Democratic	6,296,284 (41.84)	435 (81.92)	**Thomas Marshall**	Democratic
Theodore Roosevelt	Progressive	4,122,721 (27.40)	88 (16.57)	Hiram Johnson	Progressive
William Taft	Republican	3,486,242 (23.17)	8 (1.51)	Nicholas Butler	Republican
		1916 - 11/07/1916			
Woodrow Wilson	Democratic	9,126,868 (49.24)	277 (52.17)	**Thomas Marshall**	Democratic
Charles Hughes	Republican	8,548,728 (46.12)	254 (47.83)	Charles Fairbanks	Republican
		1920 - 11/02/1920			
Warren Harding	Republican	16,144,093 (60.32)	404 (76.08)	**Calvin Coolidge**	Republican
James Cox	Democratic	9,139,661 (34.15)	127 (23.92)	Franklin Roosevelt	Democratic

(*continued*)

U.S. Presidential Elections Since 1860 (Major Candidates) (*continued*)

Presidential Candidates	Party	Votes (%)	Electoral College (%)	Vice Presidential Candidates	Party
1924 - 11/04/1924					
Calvin Coolidge	Republican	15,723,789 (54.04)	382 (71.94)	**Charles Dawes**	Republican
John Davis	Democratic	8,386,242 (28.82)	136 (25.61)	Charles Bryan	Democratic
Robert LaFollette	Progressive, Socialist	4,831,706 (16.61)	13 (2.45)	Burton Wheeler	Progressive, Socialist
1928 - 11/06/1928					
Herbert Hoover	Republican	21,427,123 (58.21)	444 (83.62)	**Charles Curtis**	Republican
Alfred Smith	Democratic	15,015,464 (40.80)	87 (16.38)	Joseph Robinson	Democratic
1932 - 11/08/1932					
Franklin Roosevelt	Democratic	22,821,277 (57.41)	472 (88.89)	**John Garner**	Democratic
Herbert Hoover	Republican	15,761,254 (39.65)	59 (11.11)	Charles Curtis	Republican
1936 - 11/03/1936					
Franklin Roosevelt	Democratic	27,752,648 (60.80)	523 (98.49)	**John Garner**	Democratic
Alfred Landon	Republican	16,681,862 (36.54)	8 (1.51)	Frank Knox	Republican
1940 - 11/05/1940					
Franklin Roosevelt	Democratic	27,313,945 (54.74)	449 (84.56)	**Henry Wallace**	Democratic
Wendell Willkie	Republican	22,347,744 (44.78)	82 (15.44)	Charles McNary	Republican
1944 - 11/07/1944					
Franklin Roosevelt	Democratic	25,612,916 (53.39)	432 (81.36)	**Harry Truman**	Democratic
Thomas Dewey	Republican	22,017,929 (45.89)	99 (18.64)	John Bricker	Republican

U.S. Presidential Elections Since 1860 (Major Candidates) (*continued*)

Presidential Candidates	Party	Votes (%)	Electoral College (%)	Vice Presidential Candidates	Party
1948 - 11/02/1948					
Harry Truman	Democratic	24,179,347 (49.55)	303 (57.06)	**Alben Barkely**	Democratic
Thomas Dewey	Republican	21,991,292 (45.07)	189 (35.60)	Earl Warren	Republican
J. Strom Thurmond	States' Rights Democratic	1,175,930 (2.41)	39 (7.34)	Fielding Wright	States' Rights Democratic
1952 - 11/04/1952					
Dwight Eisenhower	Republican	34.075,529 (55.18)	442 (83.24)	**Richard Nixon**	Republican
Adlai Stevenson	Democratic	27,375,090 (44.33)	89 (16.76)	John Sparkman	Democratic
1956 - 11/06/1956					
Dwight Eisenhower	Republican	35,579,180 (57.37)	457 (86.06)	**Richard Nixon**	Republican
Adlai Stevenson	Democratic	26,028,028 (41.97)	73 (13.75)	Estes Kefauver	Democratic
1960 - 11/08/1960					
John Kennedy	Democratic	34,220,984 (49.72)	303 (56.42)	**Lyndon Johnson**	Democratic
Richard Nixon	Republican	34,108,157 (49.55)	219 (40.78)	Henry Lodge	Republican
1964 - 11/03/1964					
Lyndon Johnson	Democratic	42,127,041 (61.05)	486 (90.33)	**Hubert Humphrey**	Democratic
Barry Goldwater	Republican	27,175,754 (38.47)	52 (9.67)	William Miller	Republican
1968 - 11/05/1968					
Richard Nixon	Republican	31,783,783 (43.42)	301 (55.95)	**Spiro Agnew**	Republican

(*continued*)

U.S. Presidential Elections Since 1860 (Major Candidates) (*continued*)

Presidential Candidates	Party	Votes (%)	Electoral College (%)	Vice Presidential Candidates	Party
Hubert Humphrey	Democratic	31,271,839 (42.72)	191 (35.50)	Edmund Muskie	Democratic
George Wallace	American Independent	9,901,118 (13.53)	46 (8.55)	Curtis LeMay	American Independent
1972 - 11/07/1972					
Richard Nixon	Republican	47,168,710 (60.67)	520 (96.65)	**Spiro Agnew**	Republican
George McGovern	Democratic	29,173,222 (37.52)	17 (3.16)	Sargent Shriver	Democratic
1976 - 11/02/1976					
James Carter	Democratic	40,831,881 (50.08)	297 (55.20)	**Walter Mondale**	Democratic
Gerald Ford	Republican	39,148,634 (48.02)	240 (44.61)	Robert Dole	Republican
1980 - 11/04/1980					
Ronald Reagan	Republican	43,903,230 (50.75)	489 (90.89)	**George H. W. Bush**	Republican
James Carter	Democratic	35,480,115 (41.01)	49 (9.11)	Walter Mondale	Democratic
1984 - 11/04/1984					
Ronald Reagan	Republican	54,455,472 (58.77)	525 (97.58)	**George H. W. Bush**	Republican
Walter Mondale	Democratic	37,577,352 (40.56)	13 (2.42)	Geraldine Ferraro	Democratic
1988 - 11/08/1988					
George H. W. Bush	Republican	48,886,597 (53.37)	426 (79.18)	**Danforth Quayle**	Republican
Michael Dukakis	Democratic	41,809,476 (45.65)	111 (20.63)	Lloyd Bentsen	Democratic

U.S. Presidential Elections Since 1860 (Major Candidates) (*continued*)

Presidential Candidates	Party	Votes (%)	Electoral College (%)	Vice Presidential Candidates	Party
1992 - 11/03/1992					
William Clinton	Democratic	44,909,806 (43.01)	370 (68.77)	**Albert Gore**	Democratic
George H. W. Bush	Republican	39,104,550 (37.45)	168 (31.23)	Danforth Quayle	Republican
H. Ross Perot	Independent	19,743,821 (18.91)	0 (0.00)	James Stockdale	Independent
1996 - 11/05/1996					
William Clinton	Democratic	47,400,125 (49.23)	379 (70.45)	**Albert Gore**	Democratic
Robert Dole	Republican	39,198,755 (40.72)	159 (29.55)	Jack Kemp	Republican
2000 - 11/07/2000[2]					
George W. Bush	Republican	50,460,110 (47.87)	271 (50.37)	**Richard Cheney**	Republican
Albert Gore	Democratic	51,003,926 (48.38)	266 (49.44)	Joseph Lieberman	Democratic
Ralph Nader	Green	2,883,105 (2.73)	0 (0.00)	Winona LaDuke	Green
2004 - 11/02/2004					
George W. Bush	Republican	62,040,610 (50.73)	286 (53.16)	**Richard Cheney**	Republican
John Kerry	Democratic	59,028,439 (48.27)	251 (46.65)	John Edwards	Democratic
2008- 11/04/2008					
Barack Obama	Democratic	66,882,230 (53)	365 (68)	**Joseph Biden**	Democratic
John McCain	Republican	58,343,671 (46)	173 (32)	Sarah Palin	Republican

Note: **Bold** indicates the winner.

1. Democratic/Liberal Republican Presidential Candidate Horace Greeley died after the election and before the electors voted. His votes were scattered among others in the Democratic/Liberal Republican coalition, including to Vice Presidential candidate B. Gratz Brown.

2. The election of 2000 was the most contested of the modern age.

Sources: "Results of Presidential Elections," U.S. Constitution Online, http://www.usconstitution.net/elections.html, and www.infoplease.com, http://www.infoplease.com/ipa/A0781450.html.

SELECTED BIBLIOGRAPHY

BOOKS

Alexander, Paul. *Man of the People*. Hoboken, NJ: Wiley, 2003.

Barone, Michael. *The Almanac of American Politics, 2004*. Washington, DC: National Journal, 2003.

Barone, Michael, with Richard E. Cohen. *The Almanac of American Politics, 2002*. Washington, DC: National Journal, 2001.

Barone, Michael, and Richard E. Cohen. *The Almanac of American Politics, 2006*. Washington, DC: National Journal, 2005.

Barone, Michael, and Richard E. Cohen. *The Almanac of American Politics, 2008*. Washington, DC: National Journal, 2007.

Barone, Michael, and Grant Ujifusa. *The Almanac of American Politics, 1988*. Washington, DC: National Journal, 1987.

Barone, Michael, and Grant Ujifusa. *The Almanac of American Politics, 1990*. Washington, DC: National Journal, 1989.

Barone, Michael, and Grant Ujifusa. *The Almanac of American: Politics, 1992*. Washington, DC: National Journal, 1991.

Barone, Michael, and Grant Ujifusa. *The Almanac of American Politics, 1994*. Washington, DC: National Journal, 1993.

Barone, Michael, and Grant Ujifusa. *The Almanac of American Politics, 1996*. Washington, DC: National Journal, 1995.

Barone, Michael, and Grant Ujifusa. *The Almanac of American Politics, 1998*. Washington, DC: National Journal, 1997.

Clarke, Torie. *Lipstick on a Pig: Winning in the No Spin Era by Someone Who Knows the Game*. New York: Free Press, 2006.

Drew, Elizabeth. *Citizen McCain*. New York: Simon and Schuster, 2002.

Duncan, Phil, and the CQ Political Staff. *Congressional Quarterly's Politics in America 1988: The 100th Congress*. Washington, DC: CQ Press, 1987.

Duncan, Phil, and the CQ Political Staff. *Congressional Quarterly's Politics in America 1990: The 101st Congress*. Washington, DC: CQ Press, 1989.

Duncan, Phil, and the CQ Political Staff. *Congressional Quarterly's Politics in America 1992: The 102nd Congress*. Washington, DC: CQ Press, 1991.

Duncan, Phil, and the CQ Political Staff. *Politics in America, 1994: The 103rd Congress*. Washington, DC: CQ Press, 1993.

Duncan, Phil, and the Staff of Congressional Quarterly. *CQ's Politics in America, 1996: The 104th Congress*. Washington, DC: CQ Press, 1995.

Duncan, Phil, and Christine C. Lawrence. *CQ's Politics in America, 1998: The 105th Congress*. Washington, DC: CQ Press, 1997.

Duncan, Philip, and Brian Nutting, eds. *CQ's Politics in America 2000: The 106th Congress*. Washington, DC: CQ Press, 1999.

Ehrenhalt, Alan. *Politics in America 1984*. Washington, DC: CQ Press, 1983.

Ehrenhalt, Alan. *Politics in America 1986*. Washington, DC: Congressional Quarterly Books, 1985.

Freeman, Gregory A., *Sailors to the End: The Deadly Fire on the USS Forrestal and the Heroes Who Fought It*. New York: HarperCollins, 2002.

Halberstam, David. *The Best and the Brightest*. Greenwich, CT: Fawcett, 1969.

Hawkings, David, and Brian Nutting, eds., and Congressional Quarterly Staff. *CQ's Politics in America 2004: The 108th Congress*. Washington, DC: CQ Press, 2003.

Koszczuk, Jackie, and H. Amy Stern, eds., and the Congressional Quarterly Staff. *CQ's Politics in America, 2006: The 109th Congress*. Washington, DC: CQ Press, 2005.

McCain, John, with Mark Salter. *Faith of My Fathers*. New York: Random House, 1999.

McCain, John, with Mark Salter. *Worth the Fighting For*. New York: Random House, 2002.

McCain, John, with Mark Salter. *Why Courage Matters*. New York: Random House, 2004.

McCain, John, with Mark Salter. *Character Is Destiny*. New York: Random House, 2005.

McCain, John, with Mark Salter. *Hard Call: The Art of Great Decisions*. New York: Hachette Book Group USA, 2007.

Nutting, Brian, and H. Amy Stern, eds. *CQ's Politics in America 2002: The 107th Congress*. Washington, DC: CQ Press, 2001.

Rudman, Warren. *Combat: Twelve Years in the U.S. Senate*. New York: Random House, 1996.

Sheehan, Neil. *A Bright Shining Lie: John Paul Vann and America in Vietnam*. New York: Random House, 1988.

Timberg, Robert. *John McCain: An American Odyssey*. New York: Free Press, 1995.

Timberg, Robert. *The Nightingale's Song*. New York: Simon and Schuster, 1995.

PERIODICALS

All Hands (U.S. Navy publication)
The Congressional Record
Harper's Bazaar
National Guard Magazine
National Journal
Newsweek
U.S. News and World Report

NEWSPAPERS AND NEWS SERVICES

Arizona Daily Star
The Arizona Republic
The Associated Press
The Baltimore Sun
The Bath (Maine) Daily Times
The Boston Globe
The Los Angeles Times
Newsday
The New York Times
The Phoenix Gazette
USA Today
The Wall Street Journal
The Washington Post

WEB SITES (OTHER THAN NEWSPAPERS)

Archives of the United States, http://www.archives.gov/education/lessons/day-of-infamy/

Cuban Missile Crisis history, Global Security.org, http://www.globalsecurity.org/military/ops/cuba-62.htm

Episcopal High School Web site, http://www.episcopalhighschool.
   org/about/mccaininfo.html
The Heritage Foundation collection, http://www.reagansheritage.
   org/html/reagan_rnc_88.shtml
John McCain 2008, www.johnmccain.com
John McCain Senate Web site, http://mccain.senate.gov/public/
Massachusetts Institute of Technology, http://www.esd.mit.edu/
   people/dissertations/kometer_michael.pdf
Senate Report 103–1, "POW/MIA'S, Report of the Select Com-
   mittee on POW/MIA Affairs," U.S. Senate, January 13, 1993,
   http://www.fas.org/irp/congress/1993_rpt/pow-exec.html
University of Washington libraries, Henry M. Jackson papers, http://
   www.lib.washington.edu/specialcoll/findaids/docs/papersrecords/
   JacksonHenry3560.html
USS *Gunnel*,Second War Patrol, http://www.jmlavelle.com/gunnel/
   patrol2.htm
You Tube, "Raw Video: You Little Jerk, McCain Laughs," http://
   www.youtube.com/watch?v=F2zx3–0zOPs

BROADCAST SOURCES

CBS, *Evening News with Katie Couric*
CNN, *Political Ticker*
NBC, *Tonight Show with Jay Leno*
PBS, *The American Experience*
PBS, *Newshour with Jim Lehrer*

INDIVIDUAL INTERVIEWS

Naomi Belisle
Torie Clarke
William Cohen
Frank Gamboa
Todd Harris
John McCain
Joseph P. McCain
Roberta W. McCain
Howard Opinsky
Edward Pritchard
Morele Rosenfeld

Warren Rudman
Mark Salter
Jay Smith
Orson Swindle
Lanny Wiles

INDEX

About the Author

ELAINE S. POVICH is a prize-winning journalist who has extensive experience in writing about Congress and politics. She has covered the past 13 Congresses and the presidential elections of 1988, 1992, 1996, 2000, and 2004, writing for United Press International, the *Chicago Tribune*, and *Newsday*. She is a winner of the top prize for congressional reporting, the Everett McKinley Dirksen Award for Distinguished Reporting of Congress, as well as several other awards. She is the author of *Nancy Pelosi: A Biography* (Greenwood Publishing Group, 2008) and *Partners and Adversaries: The Contentious Connection between Congress and the Media* (1996). Povich lives with her husband, Ron Dziengiel, and two sons, Mark and Kenny Dziengiel, in Laurel, Maryland.

CPSIA information can be obtained
at www.ICGtesting.com
Printed in the USA
LVHW051024311220
675340LV00004BB/158